WALL FLOWER

A Life on the German Border

In August 1961, seventeen-year-old Rita Kuczynski was living with her grandmother and studying piano at a conservatory in West Berlin. Caught in East Berlin by the rise of the Berlin Wall while on a summer visit to her parents, she found herself trapped behind the Iron Curtain for the next twenty-eight years.

Kuczynski's fascinating memoir relates her experiences of life in East Germany as a student, a fledgling academic philosopher, an independent writer, and, above all, as a woman. Though she was never a true believer in Communism, Rita gained entry into the circles of the East German intellectual elite through her husband, Thomas Kuczynski. There, in the privileged world that she calls "the gardens of the nomenklatura," she saw first-hand the contradictions at the heart of life for the East German intelligentsia.

Published in English for the first time twenty-six years after the fall of the Berlin Wall, *Wall Flower* offers a rare – and critical – look at life among the East German elite. Told with wry wit and considerable candor, Kuczynski's story offers a fascinating perspective on the rise and fall of East Germany.

RITA KUCZYNSKI is a writer, journalist, and philosopher. The author of more than eleven books, both fiction and non-fiction, she lives and works in Berlin.

ANTHONY J. STEINHOFF is a professor in the Department of History at the Université du Québec à Montréal.

RITA KUCZYNSKI

WALL FLOWER

A Life on the German Border

Translated by Anthony J. Steinhoff

UNIVERSITY OF TORONTO PRESS
Toronto Buffalo London

Toronto Buffalo London
www.utppublishing.com

ISBN 978-1-4426-4818-0 (cloth)
ISBN 978-1-4426-1622-6 (paper)

Library and Archives Canada Cataloguing in Publication

Kuczynski, Rita
[Mauerblume. English]
Wall flower : a life on the German border / Rita Kuczynski ; translated by Anthony J. Steinhoff.

Translation of: Mauerblume.
Includes bibliographical references.
ISBN 978-1-4426-4818-0 (bound) ISBN 978-1-4426-1622-6 (paperback)

1. Kuczynski, Rita. 2. Authors, German – 20th century – Biography. 3. Elite (Social sciences) – Germany (East). 4. Germany (East) – Intellectual life – 20th century. 5. Germany (East) – Social life and customs – 20th century.
I. Steinhoff, Anthony J., translator II. Title. III. Title: Mauerblume. English.

PT2671.U27Z4613 2015 838′.91409 C2015-904153- 8

University of Toronto Press acknowledges the financial assistance to its publishing program of the Canada Council for the Arts and the Ontario Arts Council, an agency of the Government of Ontario.

Canada Council for the Arts Conseil des Arts du Canada

Funded by the Government of Canada Financé par le gouvernement du Canada Canada

For David

Contents

Translator's Foreword

Anthony J. Steinhoff

On the morning of 13 August 1961, the residents of Berlin, Germany awoke to a profound shock. The city was in the process of being physically split into two, as East German officials erected barbed wire fences, closed up houses, and set up temporary barricades all along the border between the eastern and western parts of the city. Of course, the city had been divided administratively among Britain, France, the Soviet Union, and the United States ever since July 1945. In 1949, the Soviet sector, East Berlin, became the capital of the German Democratic Republic (GDR or East Germany), while the remaining three sectors formed "West Berlin," an isolated outpost of the new Federal Republic of Germany (West Germany). Throughout the 1950s, the sense of separation across the internal Berlin border become ever more palpable. There were two municipal administrations and two distinct currencies. Postwar urban reconstruction in the two parts of the city also evolved along discrete lines. And yet, the border was still surprisingly permeable. Berliners still crossed it regularly and with relatively few restrictions: to go to work, to visit family, and to attend cultural or sporting events. As Rita Kuczynski suggests in the opening chapter of her memoir, the city's mass transit system, the S-Bahn (rapid trains) and U-Bahn (subway and elevated lines), perhaps best symbolized how Berlin's sense of itself as *one* city remained intact. For the trains continued to run from one end of the city to another, essentially ignoring the political and administrative demarcations that Cold War animosities had placed upon it.

This all changed on that fateful day in August. Acting with the full support of the Soviets, the East German head of state, Walter Ulbricht, moved to close what had been a gaping hole in the Iron Curtain and a major source of embarrassment for the East German government.

Between 1950 and 1961, hundreds of thousands of East Germans took advantage of Berlin's special status to migrate to the West. Not only did this emigration constitute a massive rejection of the socialist society Ulbricht was striving to build in East Germany, but increasingly many of those defecting were precisely the sorts of people the nascent East German state desperately needed: doctors, engineers, teachers, lawyers, farmers, and skilled workers. Indeed, for Ulbricht and the heads of the Socialist Unity Party (Sozialistische Einheitspartei Deutschlands or SED, the East German "communist" party's official name), sealing off West Berlin from the rest of East Germany was essential for the socialist state's very survival.

The creation of the Berlin Wall, as the barrier between East and West Germany soon came to be known, was without question one of the critical moments in the Cold War. It made clear that the postwar reunification of Germany would, for the foreseeable future, be but a far-off dream. For the Western public, the Wall itself quickly became a symbol of divided Europe and of the clash of the seemingly irreconcilable ideological systems of communism and capitalism. Moreover, in the days and years following the Wall's construction, East Berliners risked life and limb to escape the confines of what the East German authorities cynically termed the "antifascist protective wall" (*antifaschischter Schutzwall*). They jumped from windows, tunnelled under barriers, and hid in secret compartments of automobiles. These dramatic exploits captured the public imagination, providing the stuff for sensational news stories and documentary films. In addition, they helped to transform the Wall into the most tangible and visible sign of state socialism's assault on freedom and human rights.

Western responses to the Wall's construction and continued existence also served to underscore the ways in which Berlin's physical partition came to stand in for the postwar divisions of Germany and Europe. When the American president John F. Kennedy came to Berlin in June 1963, he did more than proudly declare himself to be a Berliner. He proclaimed the Wall to be "the most obvious and vivid sign of the failures of the communist system" and suggested that Berlin was living proof both that communism was not "the wave of the future" and that cooperation with communists in Europe was impossible.[1] Almost twenty-five years later in 1987, on the 750th anniversary of Berlin's founding, another American president, Ronald Reagan, delivered an address in which he too invoked the idea of a single Berlin ("Es gibt nur ein Berlin," "There is only one Berlin"). But he also noted, "It is here in Berlin where the wall [between East and West] emerges most clearly; here, cutting across our city, where the news photo and the television screen have imprinted this brutal division of a continent upon the mind of the world." Famously, he closed his remarks by calling on the Soviet chairman, Mikhail Gorbachev, to come to Berlin and "tear down this wall!"[2]

On 9 November 1989, the Berlin Wall did collapse. Confronted with mounting protests against the socialist system that year (and setbacks suffered earlier in the year by the communist parties in Hungary and Poland), East German authorities suddenly announced that they would permit unrestricted crossing across the internal German border, including the Berlin Wall. That evening, thousands of people flowed across the Wall, to the amazement of stunned border guards and people around the world. The rapid demise of the East German state now set in. During the free elections held in March 1990, the Party of Democratic Socialism (a reorganized version of the SED) was roundly defeated. Shortly thereafter, the new East German government voted to demolish the Wall. On 18 May, the two German states concluded a treaty that provided for the introduction of the West German mark (*Deutschmark*) into East Germany and East Germany's incorporation into the Federal Republic. After the currency union took effect on 1 July and the East German parliament (Volkskammer) ratified the unification treaty on 20 September, everything was set for the GDR's disappearance, which duly occurred on 3 October. The events in Berlin also provided the signal to call off the socialist experiments elsewhere in Eastern Europe, from Poland to Bulgaria. In the summer of 1991, hardliners in the Soviet Union sought to turn back the clock by staging a coup d'état against Gorbachev, whose policies of restructuring (*perestroika*) and openness (*glasnost*) had fatally undermined state socialism in Eastern Europe. Although the coup failed, the days of Gorbachev's career and the Soviet Union were clearly numbered. Gorbachev announced his retirement as president of the Soviet Union on 25 December; one day later the Soviet Union was formally dissolved.

Rita Kuczynski's memoir *Mauerblume* (literally, "Wall Flower") was published in German on the tenth anniversary of the Berlin Wall's collapse. It relates Kuczynski's experiences in Berlin during the years of division, with special emphasis on the period following the Wall's construction, as well as during the decade following the city's reunification. As specialists in East German history are well aware, this decade was rich in terms of "autobiographical production." One after another, a number of former East German leading lights – noted authors (e.g.,

Günter de Bruyn and Christa Wolf); leading academics (Fritz Klein, the director of the Institute of History in the Academy of Sciences, and Kuczynski's father-in-law, the economic historian Jürgen Kuczynski); and even Markus Wolff, the former head of East Germany's foreign espionage service – felt compelled to publish accounts of their lives in what had been the GDR.[3]

In two respects, *Mauerblume* rates as a rather exceptional contribution to this spate of autobiographical writing. First, unlike most of her peers writing in the genre and despite her famous last name, Rita Kuczynski was herself a relatively unknown figure. Apart from a study of Hegel, *Nächte mit Hegel* (Nights with Hegel, 1984), her freelance efforts resulted in the publication of a pair of novels (*Wenn ich kein Vögel war/ If I Were Not a Bird*, 1990; and *staccato*, 1997), but neither was widely reviewed. Second, there is a considerable difference in the authors' respective autobiographical imperatives. Most of the autobiographers found the writing of memoirs after 1989 to be doubly congenial: it enabled them to continue exercising their former function as shapers of public opinion while also giving them a forum through which they could explain and justify their actions and ties to the now defunct GDR regime. Neither of these considerations, however, pertained to Kuczynski's situation, precisely because of her status as a relatively "average" East German. In fact, she initially had no intention of publishing her story. That *Mauerblume* even materialized stems from the prompting of one of her lodgers, the American historian David Schoenbaum, who insisted and ultimately convinced Kuczynski that her account of her experiences in Berlin warranted publication. The decision to prepare an English translation of *Mauerblume*, the first translation of the work in any language, is in keeping with Schoenbaum's assessment: not only is this a good story, but it is one that offers new opportunities for thinking about and understanding what had been East Berlin and East Germany.

The era of state socialism in Eastern Europe, running from 1945 to 1989, occupies a major piece of what the British historian E.J. Hobsbawm once described as Europe's "short" twentieth century, that is, Europe since 1918.[4] And yet, it is fair to say that it still occupies a rather marginal place in our historical consciousness, particularly if the "we" here is defined as the general public of Western Europe and North America. This is not at all to state that this history is unknown. To the contrary. Scholars working in a number of disciplines – history, political science, sociology, literature, cultural studies, for instance – have subjected the period to considerable scrutiny over the past few decades, and, on a number of levels, their research has succeeded in lifting the veil of disinformation and secrecy that once shrouded the several people's democracies.[5] Research into the East German past has been an especially productive field of activity, aided by exceptional access to the archives of the former GDR state and its institutions after 1989. It has also been encouraged by debates (and occasional controversy) over how to write that past and relate it to the present.

Of course, in one way or another, all states of the former Soviet bloc have had to come to terms with the events of the communist era. In the course of their often messy transition out of state socialism, they have had to negotiate what to retain, what to remember, and, no less important, what to forget. The fact that the GDR no longer exists, however, has made the internal German discussion about the period 1945–89 unique, since inclusion in the Federal Republic effectively ruled out the option of holding on to pieces of the former socialist system. The triumphalist position of individuals like the noted West German historian Hans-Ulrich Wehler, who controversially contended that the "short-lived GDR was only 'a footnote in world history,'" is admittedly extreme.[6] But it raises a fundamental question all the same: where *does* the history of this "ghost state" fit within the narratives of Germany's post-1945 past?[7] That is, how can we conceive of an integrated history of a divided country? How do we understand not just the GDR's collapse but also its significant longevity? The GDR's forty years of existence, after all, long surpassed the twelve-year lifespan of Adolf Hitler's "one thousand year" Reich. Finally, how do we "read" the GDR so as to avoid the simplifications present both in Wehler's assertion and in what has come to be called *Ostalgie* ("nostalgia for the East")? Here it makes most sense to see *Ostalgie* as an inclination on the part of some East Germans to view the GDR past through rose-coloured glasses, remembering certain benefits of the system (e.g., guaranteed employment, child care, subsidized housing, access to cultural activities) while downplaying (and even overlooking) its shortcomings: from constant shortages and restrictions on education, employment, and movement to pervasive surveillance and bouts of real repression.

Describing East Germany's place in our historical consciousness as marginal should also not be understood to denote a lack of interest. On both sides of the Atlantic, evidence of considerable curiosity about the former East Bloc and its inhabitants abounds. University students on North American and British campuses, for example, eagerly enrol in courses on Eastern Germany and Eastern Europe. Films such as Wolfgang Becker's *Good-bye Lenin!* (2003) and Florian Henckel von Donnersmarck's *The Lives of Others* (*Das Leben der Anderen*, 2006) have played well in non-German theatres; the latter even won the 2006 Academy Award for the Best Foreign Film. Moreover, books on the Berlin Wall (e.g., Frederick Taylor's *The Berlin Wall: A World Divided, 1961–1989* and Peter Schneider's *The Wall Jumper*), the East German intelligence service (Stasi) (e.g., Anna Funder's *Stasiland: Stories from behind the Berlin Wall*), and also Markus Wolff's memoir, *Man without a Face*, have attracted a considerable readership. Last but certainly not least, each year streams of tourists visit such sites in Berlin as the Wall Memorial and the Checkpoint Charlie and DDR Museums.

Nevertheless, the public image of what life was like behind the Wall is still more attuned to the ideological dichotomies that prevailed during the Cold War than it is to the shades of grey evoked in more recent scholarly research. Accordingly, communism – one speaks rarely of socialism, the term preferred in the East – is presented as a dictatorial system that denied individuals their freedoms and human rights. The walls and fortified borders that made up the Iron Curtain, ostensibly created to protect citizens from Western capitalism and exploitation, in fact served to transform the people's democracies into prisons: citizens were not free to leave the country, and frequently even movement within the country was subject to restrictions. Similarly, the representations produced by the media and by museums have tended to accentuate the difficulties of everyday life under socialism. Not only do they chronicle the persecution of opposition and dissent and the ubiquity of state surveillance measures, but they also highlight the drudgery of daily existence and the absence of meaningful choices, whether political, social, or economic. Unquestionably, these elements form a crucial part of the narrative. They help us to understand why the socialist regimes collapsed at the end of the 1980s. They also help to legitimate the turns towards democracy and a market economy after 1989. But in its simplification of actually complex and complicated situations, the recounting of this era in black and white obstructs efforts to comprehend how the socialist states operated, how people made do, and, perhaps most importantly, why many long believed that Eastern-style state socialism was a viable alternative to Western-style democracy and capitalism. Herein lies a major strength of the narrative Rita Kuczynski offers in *Mauerblume*. Although her story, too, charts the travails of daily life under socialism, it does so in a way that permits the reader, even one with some familiarity with the GDR, to take note of and reflect on the system's ambiguities as well as the spaces it created, however unintentionally, for a certain (if also varying) degree of autonomous action.

As the reader will discover, much of this memoir's appeal stems from Kuczynski's literary talent and the peculiarities of her particular circumstances. In the very presentation of the story, she underscores its idiosyncratic character. With the book's main German title, "Mauerblume," she presents herself as a flower on the (Berlin) Wall, an image that evokes a sense of survival amidst difficult conditions. In addition, she gives her account the subtitle "Ein Leben auf der Grenze" ("A Life on the Border"), with "border" being conceived both in the literal sense of the Wall and also figuratively, denoting the internal German divide that existed in Berlin both before 1961 and after 1989. The use of the singular "A" here is also significant. It makes explicit Kuczynski's position that she is only telling one person's story, without making claims to be representative of anyone else's experiences, whether other writers, other philosophers, or even other women. If partly an expression of Kuczynski's own modesty and initial reluctance to set down her story on paper, this admission of the singularity of her experiences reminds us too of the subjectivities inherent in the autobiographical genre. Subjective, first and foremost, because it is the author's memories – her perspectives – that are recounted in the text. But subjective too in that memory is fallible. Thus, even when there is no evidence of deliberate effort to distort or rewrite the past, we as readers must continually keep in mind the incompleteness and constructedness of the record that memoirs and similar texts present.

In preparing the English translation of *Mauerblume*, it seemed particularly desirable to render the title literally, thus "Wall Flower." Above all, this permits an allusion to the English word "wallflower," a notion that adroitly captures an important dimension of *Mauerblume*'s value as a window onto the East German past. For just as the "typical" wallflower is present at dances but fails to participate because too shy or awkward to be asked to the floor, so too is Rita Kuczynski more an observer than an active participant in the world around her, largely because she rarely felt that she "fit" into that world. She is, however, an adept observer. And as a result of rather fortuitous circumstances, she finds herself at many important "dances," having gained admission into some of the most intimate circles of the East German elite. Thus, while constantly clinging to her self-perception as an outsider, she affords us valuable glimpses into the world and world views of those privileged few.

The initial chapters of *Mauerblume* help establish Rita's sense of being an outsider *tout court*.[8] Life with her parents and siblings, she avows, was never easy. Her mother was more interested in proving her devotion to the socialist cause than tending to the family, which in the mid-1950s resulted in Rita being sent to live with her maternal grandmother in West Berlin. This promising existence, however, was quickly extinguished by the Berlin Wall, whose construction commenced just after Rita started her obligatory summer visit with her parents in the East. As she notes on multiple occasions, the forced captivity behind the Wall destroyed her; only after many long, painful years was she able to construct another life that was at least bearable. With brutal candour, but also wry humour, she describes the challenges of surviving behind the Wall, with barely any familial assistance, as she passed from her late teenage years into her early twenties. We see her efforts to find and keep a job, a requirement of all East German citizens, sensing also how temperamentally ill-suited she is for the posts available to her at the time. One can only imagine how many other East Berliners and East Germans found themselves in similar situations after August 1961.

Rita's determination to study philosophy at university, first in Leipzig, then in East Berlin, sets in motion the chain of events that leads to her becoming an insider, complete with her own special file in the VIP section of the Stasi archives. It was typical of her naïveté at the time, she concedes, that she didn't realize that the philosophy program was no longer about contemplating such figures as Kant, Nietzsche, or Hegel, the philosopher who really captivated her. Rather, it was the ideological training course for the GDR's future functionaries and apologists. An early turning point in Rita's narrative comes with her reunion with her former childhood friend, Esther, at Berlin's Humboldt University. Through Esther, Rita makes the acquaintance of an important group of students whom she calls the "antifascist hero-children." Important, because they are the progeny of the East German state's founders, men and women who survived the horrors of Nazi rule. They believe in socialism and the righteousness of the state's policies, not because of state propaganda or their enjoyment of special privileges, but because they are personally and intellectually convinced that socialism is the better way to the future. Rita's contact with Esther and, more specifically, Esther's father, Jonas, the chief of the East German police (the Volkspolizei), would also prove crucial to Rita's academic future. For in order to receive her philosophy degree, she had to be admitted to the SED, and this she managed only through Jonas's multiple interventions and coaching.

For us readers, the encounters between Rita and the hero-children (and, *in absentia*, their parents) are also valuable. In particular, they reveal the presence and viewpoints of a key group of individuals who earnestly believed in the system and eagerly sought to help "build socialism" and realize its potential. Of course, it is evident from Rita's account that even those most committed to socialism recognized certain of its shortcomings. But to the bitter end they continued to maintain that it wasn't the theory, but rather the practice, that was imperfect. Although Rita can never reconcile herself to this way of thinking, it is a perspective of considerable importance for understanding the longevity of the East Bloc regimes. As recent research has stressed, armed force and repression, however critical, represented only two ingredients in the complicated recipe that enabled state socialism to endure for more than forty years.[9]

The hero-children and their families provide Rita – and *Mauerblume*'s readers – with further food for thought, namely the place of Jews and Jewishness in the GDR. Soon after she starts spending time with these youths, Rita is startled to realize that the vast majority of them are from Jewish families. This is startling to her, not so much because of *their* Jewishness, but rather because it represents *her* first conscious encounter with Jews and Jewishness – on either side of divided Berlin. At the same time, Rita finds herself increasingly fascinated by Judaism and by the curious relationship between Jews and the GDR's regime; ultimately she devotes considerable attention to both over the course of *Mauerblume*'s pages. In certain respects, Rita's initial response to the hero-children's Jewish background reflects the decimated state of the German Jewish community. Berlin's postwar Jewish population was itself minuscule. In 1950 there were only some 6700 Jews in all of Berlin (0.2 per cent of the total population), in contrast to the some 160,000 Jews resident there in 1933. Moreover, the anti-Semitism accompanying the Stalinist purges of 1952 and early 1953 prompted the flight of many Jewish families and community leaders from East to West Berlin. But we can also read her surprise as another consequence of her youthfulness and political naïveté. That individuals of Jewish background were overrepresented in the ranks of the GDR's political and intellectual elite (and also in dissident circles) was widely known at the time. Admittedly, few of these public figures – including such personalities as Politburo and Central Committee member Albert Norden (1955–79); Klaus Gysi, who served as minister for culture (1967–73) and later as state secretary for religious affairs (1979–88); the writers Stephan Hermlin and Anna Seghers; as well as filmmaker *cum* dissident Jurek Becker and singer-songwriter-dissident Wolf Biermann – practised the Jewish faith. For there, the SED's position was consistent: religious convictions of any kind, Protestant, Catholic, or Jewish, were not welcome among Party members. Coming from a Jewish background, however, was not in and of itself incompatible with Party membership or even exercising important Party and state functions.

For some, Rita Kuczynski's reflections on East German Jews and their politico-cultural identities will merely add nuance to a topic that has already received considerable attention in the scholarly literature.[10] But, given the dearth of public awareness on this subject, especially circa 2014, most readers will probably be as surprised as Rita was to discover the existence of prominent Jewish communists in East Germany and East Berlin. Her comments, though, do much more than call attention to a Jewish presence in post-Holocaust East Germany. They amount to a sensitive and insightful analysis of the very meaning and articulation of a Jewish identity in the context of state socialism. That Rita is able to open this line of inquiry and thought within the context of *Mauerblume*, thereby inviting the reader to follow up on many of the points and details she raises, is in part the result of the significant role that Esther plays in Rita's story. But it is also an upshot of the most consequential accidental meeting of her life: a late night encounter with the man who became her husband, Thomas Kuczynski.

There is considerable irony in the fact that Rita not only married one of the Jewish hero-children but also through this union joined one of the leading families of the East German intelligentsia. Thomas's father was Jürgen Kuczynski (1904–1997), one of the GDR's most prominent Marxist intellectuals and a prolific and well-respected economic and labour historian, who in 1937 had left Nazi Germany for exile in England. As the reader learns, Rita does not initially react well to the news that she has become, through marriage, a sort of insider, ruing the fact that she had neglected to learn more about Thomas's background before they were married. And yet, as she also acknowledges, this marriage effectively saves her. It provides her with a sense of family that she never had. The family's access to privileges, in particular quality medical care, enables her to deal with and eventually overcome her clinical depression. Furthermore, by the end of the 1970s, she feels confident enough to exploit these very "insider" privileges to achieve greater distance from the regime, indeed to become more of a wallflower. In particular, she manages to quit her post at the Academy of Sciences, without repercussions, and become a freelance writer. With this status, she is also free of two fundamental mechanisms of citizen surveillance and control in the GDR: employee associations and Party-sponsored trade unions (she was, of course, never fully free of the third, the Stasi).

Rita describes her years with Thomas and the Kuczynski family as a time spent in the "gardens of the nomenklatura," an apt metaphor for the privileged world of East Germany's elite. Although these gardens were not Eden, they were as close to "paradise" as the East German state could offer. It is precisely her status as a wallflower, as the outsider as insider, which makes her reflections here so insightful. With her access to these gardens and that world, she is able to provide rare glimpses into the goings-on there. And while she made occasional use of her special privileges as part of that milieu, she never identified with it. This critical stance, free of apparent apologetics, helps to set *Mauerblume* apart from the memoirs and reflections written and published after 1989 by those more deeply implicated in the system, including those of her own father-in-law.[11]

And yet, we must at the same time be cautious about regarding *Mauerblume, prima facie*, as more objective or more "truthful" than these other accounts. However much Rita Kuczynski strove to retain her status as a wallflower, as an outsider, her very presence in the gardens of the nomenklatura and her recourse to certain of the privileges owing to her family status entailed making certain compromises. To be sure, the compromises, at least the ones mentioned in the narrative, did not bring her position, fame, or influence. They did, however, assure her considerable personal security and, in time, a measure of personal freedom, which were both highly valued "commodities" in the GDR. In short, for all her problems with the GDR and her conviction that it was both intellectually and, by the 1980s, economically bankrupt, Rita had succeeded in "working the system" to her own considerable advantage. But rather than conclude from these musings that we should be suspicious of her story, it makes more sense to regard the occasional blind spots and silences as part of the subjectivities inherent in autobiographical practice. Indeed, Rita Kuczynski's own situation reveals GDR society to have been curiously feudal. Just as was true in pre-Revolutionary France, privilege did not just set the GDR elite off from everyone else in society, it defined relations at every level of GDR society. In useful ways, thus, the vagueness of Kuczynski's position (and even her accounting of it) calls attention to the very complexities and ambiguities of social relationships in GDR.

There is one final perspective onto life behind the Wall and in reunified Berlin that emerges from *Mauerblume* that warrants mention here, namely, the status of women. Kuczynski herself is reluctant to frame her story in such gendered terms. Only in the final chapters (notably 16 and 18) does she address the question directly and then only in response to the changes in the former East following the Wall's collapse. Nevertheless, it is hard to avoid seeing this memoir as a contribution to a women's history of the GDR, a *herstory*. In this respect, *Mauerblume* warrants comparison with the accounts of two other Eastern European women whose accounts of life under socialism have been well received in their English-language translations, namely Heda Margolius Kovaly's *Under a Cruel Star: A Life in Prague 1941–1968* and Slavenka Drakulic's *How We Survived Communism and Even Laughed*. Rita did not just struggle with the "system" simply as a citizen; she did so as a woman. Time and again, her story shows that the GDR's official rhetoric about gender equality failed to change the deeply patriarchal and even misogynist nature of East German society. This is evident in Rita's turbulent relations with her father and in the (menial) employment options she is offered following her release from psychiatric care. On her arrival at the Academy of Sciences, the staff regards her as a little girl; only her marriage – and not her intellectual abilities – will secure her position there and offer her a general degree of protection from the "system." Finally, at the same time that the Kuczynski family provided her with emotional and financial support, it expected her to support Thomas in his career: procuring his suits and ties, organizing social gatherings, and playing the role of the *salonfähig* (presentable) wife.

Furthermore, for all Rita's references in *Mauerblume* to the important men in her life – her first husband, Alex, the various father figures (Jonas; certain professors at Leipzig and Berlin; Jürgen Kuczynski; her Chilean lover, Claude), and her second husband, Thomas – her narrative is even more evocative of feminine sociability, and not just in the GDR. Indeed, the story is rich in accounts of Rita's friendships and relationships with other women: Esther, of course, but also her friend Maria at the Narva Light Bulb Factory, Alex's sister (for whom Rita never provides a name), her colleagues Carla and Reni at the Academy of Sciences, and her mother-in-law (Marguerite Kuczynski, although here too Rita never names her directly). Moreover, the more confident and self-assured Rita becomes, the wider she draws her circle of female friends and associates. In addition to engaging a female literary agent and a female tax advisor, for instance, her new-found West German friends (at least those mentioned in *Mauerblume*) are almost exclusively women. Again, while we must be wary of transforming Rita into a "representative" East German woman, a notion she would reject out of hand, the centrality of women's lives and experiences in her narrative nonetheless raises important issues about the status of women in the GDR and the types of coping mechanisms they used to deal with the gender-specific challenges and stresses produced by state socialism.

Over and above its merits for reflecting on and grappling with East Germany's past (and to a lesser degree the opening years of German reunification), *Mauerblume* is a remarkable story that Kuczynski tells beautifully. Her narrative of events is recounted in a prose style that is at once simple, lyrical, and deeply engaging. She finds humour in situations that, at heart, are anything but humorous. Her observations and reflections frequently betray the influence of her nights with Hegel, but also the lingering effects of hours at the piano and on the organ bench with Johann Sebastian Bach. Although Kuczynski insists that this is a memoir and not a work of literature, it is precisely her text's literary qualities that draw us into her story and help us as readers to imagine and contemplate this critical era in Germany's and Europe's twentieth-century histories.

Notes

1 John F. Kennedy, speech at West Berlin City Hall, 26 June 1963; full text of speech: http://millercenter.org/president/speeches/detail/3376.

2 Ronald Reagan, speech at the Berlin Reichstag, 12 June 1987; full text of speech: www.historyplace.com/speeches/reagan-tear-down.htm.

3 On the post-1989 autobiographical trend, see (among others) James R. Reece, "Remember the GDR: Memory and Evasion in Autobiographical Writing from the Former GDR," in *Textual Responses to German Unification: Processing Historical and Social Change in Literature and Film*, ed. Carol Anne Costabile-Heming, Rachel J. Halverson, and Kristie A. Foell (Berlin: de Gruyter, 2001), 59–75; and Christiane Lahusen, "Autobiography as Participation in the 'Master Narrative': GDR Academics after Unification," in *Remembering the German Democratic Republic: Divided Memory in a United Germany*, ed. David Clarke and Ute Wölfel (Basingstoke: Palgrave Macmillan, 2011), 182–94.

4 Eric J. Hobsbawm, *The Age of Extremes: The Short Twentieth Century, 1914–1991* (London: Michael Joseph, 1994).

5 For a good overview of the state of current research into the East German past, see Andrew Port, "Introduction: The Banalities of East German Historiography," in *Becoming East German: Socialist Structures and Sensibilities after Hitler*, ed. Mary Fulbrook and Andrew I. Port (New York: Berghahn Books, 2013), 1–32.
6 Hans-Ulrich Wehler, *Deutsche Gesellschaftsgeschichte*, vol. 5: *Bundesrepublik und DDR, 1949–1990* (Munich: Beck, 2008), 361.
7 See also the reflections of the American historian Donna Harsch, "Footnote or Footprint? The German Democratic Republic in History," *Bulletin of the GHI* (Washington, DC), no. 46 (Spring 2010): 9–25.
8 Since, at this point in her life, Rita is not yet a Kuczynski and she intentionally refrains from mentioning her family name, it seemed more appropriate to refer to her only by her first name.
9 See, for instance, the essays in Konrad Jarausch, ed., *Dictatorship as Experience: Towards a Socio-Cultural History of the GDR* (New York: Berghahn Books, 1999), as well as Mary Fulbrook, *The People's State: East German Society from Hitler to Honecker*, esp. part 3, "Participatory Dictatorship" (New Haven: Yale University Press, 2005), 235–90.
10 On the topic of Jews and Judaism in the GDR, see especially Robin Ostow, *Jews in Contemporary East Germany: The Children of Moses in the Land of Marx* (Basingstoke: Palgrave Macmillan, 1989); Jeffrey Herf, *Divided Memory: The Nazi Past in the Two Germanys* (Cambridge, MA: Harvard University Press, 1997), esp. 106–62; Pól Ó Dochartaigh, *The Portrayal of Jews in GDR Prose Fiction* (Amsterdam/Atlanta: Rodopi, 1997); and Jay Howard Geller, *Jews in Post-Holocaust Germany, 1945–1953* (Cambridge/New York: Cambridge University Press, 2005), esp. 160–84.
11 Jürgen Kuczynski, *Ein linientreuer Dissident: Memoiren, 1945–1989* (Berlin: Aufbau-Verlag, 1994).

Note On The Translation

Every act of translation represents an effort at making the strange familiar, and this notion certainly applies to the present work too. At a linguistic level, my goal throughout has been to capture as much of Rita Kuczynski's German prose style as possible – the sarcasm, black humour and play on words; the penchant for musical and philosophical analogies; the recourse to turns of phrase specific to the GDR era – while still producing a fluid, fully idiomatic English text. Nevertheless, in order to help situate *Mauerblume* in its specific time and place, a fair number of German words still mark the pages of *Wall Flower*. The German names of important GDR organizations and institutions (and, frequently, their acronyms), for instance, have generally been provided alongside their English translations. Most names of places and streets, however, have been kept in German (thus, Vineta Strasse, not Vineta Street), although in a few instances, an English translation has been provided along with the German (for example, Berlin *Mitte*, Central Berlin). In cases were a German word or term did not allow an easy translation into English, the German word/term is also provided within parentheses.

A memoir like *Mauerblume*, however, presents a further challenge to the translator: how to help the reader make sense of the numerous references to significant people, events, literary or artistic works, and even aspects of daily life in the GDR that figure, at times prominently, in the text. On occasion, it has been possible to provide such information by incorporating it directly into the text. Most frequently, though, these explanatory comments have been provided in the form of notes that appear at the end of the translation. Throughout the text, the existence of an explanatory comment is denoted by an asterisk. I have opted for endnotes over footnotes primarily to encourage a reading experience that most closely parallels that which the original German text offered. Above all, I hoped to avoid giving the impression, which the recourse to footnotes would have encouraged, that *Wall Flower* was some sort of scholarly autobiography.

In the course of translating *Mauerblume*, I have benefited from the generosity of a number of individuals. While they can never be fully repaid, I would like to acknowledge these debts here. Margaret E. Menninger first brought this wonderful book to my attention on a long ago summer day in Berlin and has offered numerous bits of advice on the manuscript all along the way. In addition to graciously allowing me to translate her work, Rita Kuczynski kindly responded to numerous of my emails in which I asked for clarification of particular spots in the text. For their extensive assistance with the actual translation work, I am especially grateful to Jay Feist and Linda Gaus. Thanks too to Kevin Amidon for his assistance rendering a few of *Mauerblume*'s more philosophically minded passages into quality English prose. Finally, the watchful eyes of Astrid Eckert, Joe Perry, Brian Vick, and the three anonymous readers of the manuscript for the University of Toronto Press helped rescue the text of *Wall Flower* from a number of factual blunders and linguistic infelicities, for which I am also most appreciative.

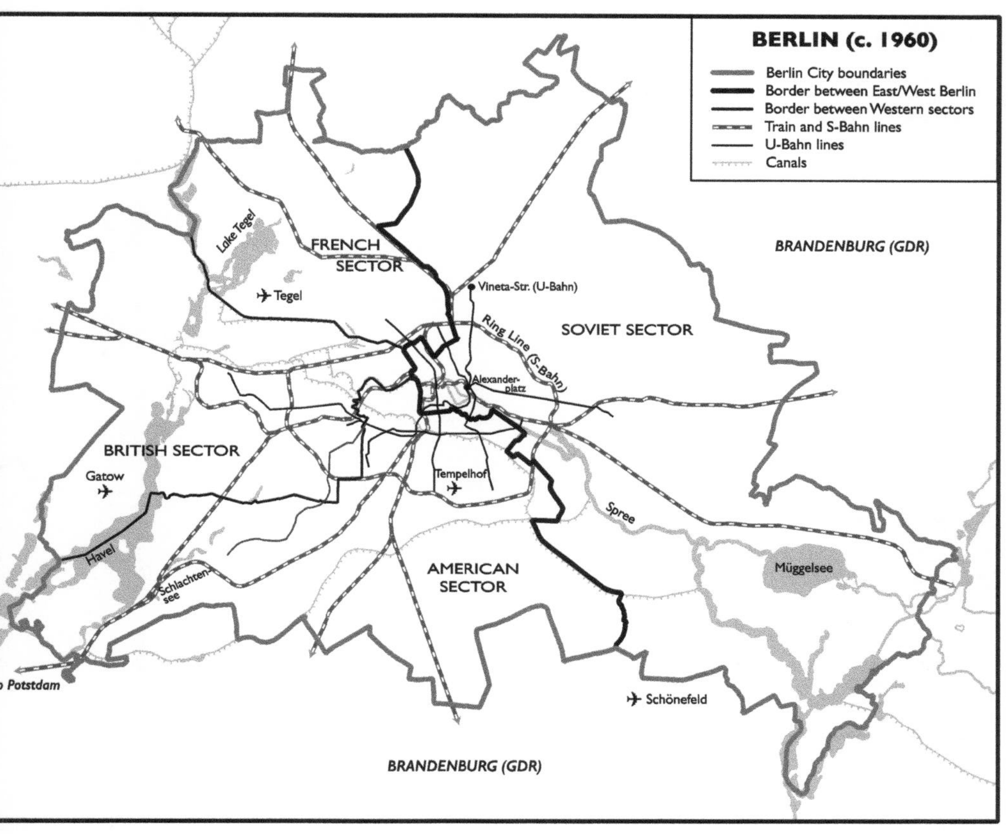
BERLIN (c. 1960)
Berlin City boundaries
Border between East/West Berlin
Border between Western sectors
Train and S-Bahn lines
U-Bahn lines
Canals
BRANDENBURG (GDR)
Lake Tegel
FRENCH SECTOR
Tegel
Vineta-Str. (U-Bahn)
Ring Line (S-Bahn)
SOVIET SECTOR
Alexanderplatz
BRITISH SECTOR
Gatow
Tempelhof
Spree
Havel
Schlachtensee
AMERICAN SECTOR
Müggelsee
to Potsdam
Schönefeld
BRANDENBURG (GDR)

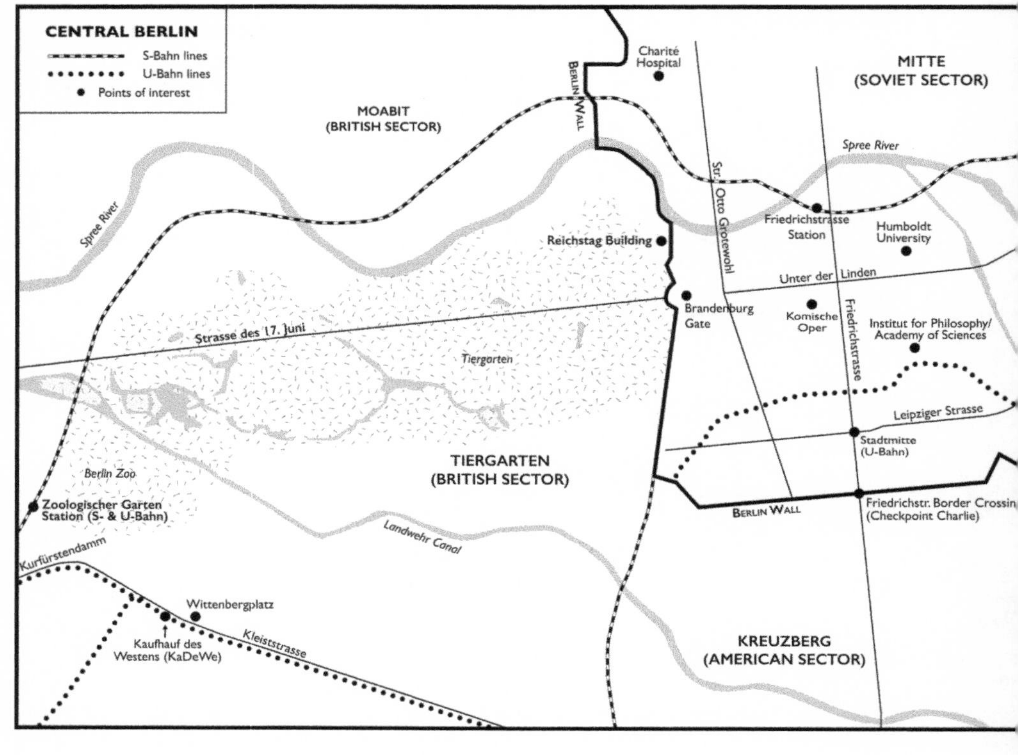
CENTRAL BERLIN
S-Bahn lines
U-Bahn lines
Points of interest
MOABIT
(BRITISH SECTOR)
Berlin Wall
Charité
Hospital
MITTE
(SOVIET SECTOR)
Spree River
Spree River
Str. Otto Grotewohl
Friedrichstrasse
Station
Humboldt
University
Reichstag Building
Unter der Linden
Brandenburg
Gate
Komische
Oper
Friedrichstrasse
Institut for Philosophy/
Academy of Sciences
Strasse des 17. Juni
Tiergarten
Leipziger Strasse
Stadtmitte
(U-Bahn)
TIERGARTEN
(BRITISH SECTOR)
Berlin Zoo
Zoologischer Garten
Station (S- & U-Bahn)
Berlin Wall
Friedrichstr. Border Crossin
(Checkpoint Charlie)
Landwehr Canal
Kurfürstendamm
Wittenbergplatz
Kaufhauf des
Westens (KaDeWe)
Kleiststrasse
KREUZBERG
(AMERICAN SECTOR)

WALL FLOWER

A Life on the German Border

I

Around the table, my mother often mentioned how I was a true "furlough child"; my sister too. By this she meant that had my father not come home on leave from the front in June 1943, I would not have been born in February 1944. In the event that he fell in the war, she at least wanted something to remember my father by. My sister came into the world two years earlier. On account of his special bravery during an assault, my father had immediately received ten days' furlough. And since Father could have been shot already in 1942, my mother wanted a souvenir of him even then. My sister and I, thus, are not just furlough children. We are also "souvenir children." When our father came back from the war, we were called war children. My two younger siblings, who were born after Father returned, became postwar children.

I later accused my mother of having pretty irresponsible reasons for bearing children. At least, as far as they concerned me. After all, by 1943 war had finally come to Germany. My mother knew nighttime bombings, and not just from hearsay. That was, I thought, hardly a time for bringing children into the world. My mother always reacted to my views about having children with a smile of superiority: it was love, she said, but I would not know anything about that.

I knew the "hot war"* only from stories. It was often discussed at family celebrations. Father spoke a lot about Stalingrad and the Eastern front, about hunger and being a Russian prisoner of war. Uncle Fred, on the other hand, told of the Western front and the French internment camps. The stories repeated themselves. As a child I was soon well informed about the encirclement of Stalingrad. But it actually did not interest me much. In addition to this, Father played "hot war" with us and the "Russian attack on the German field hospital." For that, I had to form a medical platoon with my siblings. That meant that we built stretchers for the wounded from the kitchen chairs by tying the backs of the chairs together with string. One after another we lay down on the stretchers and Father and his helper carried us through the apartment, and in summertime even across the courtyard. The less time our company needed to flee the Russians, the better prepared we were for the emergency and, accordingly, we received many pieces of toffee. My mother did not like our game. But she could not win out over Father. She never could win out over him.

When I was a child, I never really understood who won the war. The Russians? The Americans? The French and the British were discussed less. I could not understand at all what was meant by "victorious powers." When I grew up, I learned that views on victory were divided. Sometimes they depended on the part of the city where the discussion took place. In the American sector of Berlin, one heard and read that without the American army everything would have turned out much worse than it did anyway, not just for Berlin, but for Germany in general. In the Russian-occupied zone, however, one heard that the Americans had ruined everything. But that is something else I did not understand as a child.

Within the family, opinions were not just divided about victory. There were also divided opinions about the war that had been lost, which reflected the views of the conquered Germans. Uncle Richard contended that if Hitler had not been surrounded by incompetent generals, we would not have lost the war. Then a German would not have to be ashamed of himself today, nor stand around like an idiot. Then he, the German, would not have to let himself be bossed around, neither by Ivan nor by Jimmy Black.* That was Uncle Richard's honest opinion. And he knew full well that he actually was not allowed to give it. So, he expressed these deepest convictions of his only when drunk. My mother then interrupted him: Stop saying such stuff, Richard. What if someone were to hear you? Most of the time she then placed the schnapps bottle out of his reach. Then Uncle Richard, too, quieted down. But not without also saying: It's the truth. At that he tipped back his schnapps, followed it with a swig of beer, and looked out into a distance that was impossible for me to reach.

Frankly, the stories from the hot war really did not interest me much when I was a child. I had my own and these were connected with the Cold War. I grew up in a divided city: the headquarters for the four victorious powers. Each one controlled its own sector of Berlin and had its own military presence there. For just a few cents, I could travel through all four sectors on Berlin's S-Bahn:* Attention, Attention, the American sector ends here. You are now leaving the French sector, and so on. At some point the station announcement changed: Now it said I was leaving the "democratic sector" of Greater Berlin. If I travelled long enough, a voice reminded me: Attention, Attention, I was now leaving the "free sector" of Berlin.

What did I know of all this? I accepted it just like any kid. I took the free and unfree sectors for granted. Berlin, the frontline city, was my city. Almost all my relatives lived in Berlin, albeit in different sectors, which meant that the views on free and unfree shifted in their meaning. I got used to it, though. So, going back and forth between two worlds was a natural part of my life. Border between East and West, demarcation line in the Cold War. Friend and foe changed from one S-Bahn station to another.

There was one S-Bahn line that was called the "Berlin Ring." What was special about the Ring was that it had no terminus. The train ran in an endless loop through the occupied city's four sectors. The Berlin S-Bahn Ring-Line was my favourite. Now and again I rode for hours from the free to the unfree, and then back into the free part of the city. I believe that I first gained a sense of distance to East and West during my journeys on the Berlin Ring Line. In these journeys there was something of the carnival fair, the favourite playgrounds of my childhood: riding the carousel or the roller coaster with their sparkly lights. Only that with the Ring Line, I could decide the number of rounds for myself and, hence, when I wanted to get off, as well as whether I wanted to leave the station in a free or the unfree part of the city. As the basis for the decision about free or unfree, I used the place where I boarded the Ring-Line train. I accepted as given the prevailing views about freedom of that sector's occupying power. In this way, by playing I learned to handle definitions long before the subject was discussed in math class. The naturalness with which I later could navigate within the defined spaces of philosophy was also related to my life in the divided city and the constant shift in the meaning of "true" and "false," "free" and "unfree." I accepted the change in values and their determinability as something normal.

Among the most important words of my childhood were "friend" and "foe," though people talked about the foe more than the friend. This did not occur to me, however, until much later. I remember that in West Berlin I heard next to nothing about the friend; at any rate, nothing that stuck in my mind. In East Berlin, the "new Soviet man" was extolled as our friend. But since I did not know any "Soviet men" personally, these "friends" were no concern of mine.

I heard more about the foe, or enemy. The enemy, I soon learned, was organized locally. Sometimes he appeared within the family. By which I mean: If I stopped in East Berlin, my maternal grandfather (or Westopa) was an enemy because he was in the Christian Democratic Party* and, thereby, supported the Americans. If I stopped in West Berlin, my grandfather in the East (or Ostopa) was now an enemy since he organized for the Socialist Unity Party (SED)* and was pro-Russian. Had my Westopa not always been somewhat afraid of my grandmother, he would even have called my mother an enemy, since she was also in the SED. But he did not dare do that. Instead, he hated my Ostopa more than necessary. I mean, my Ostopa simply received my mother's portion along with his own. But I could not believe in the enemy. I could not care less about the enemy.

With my sister I trained for the hot war at home. I called it the "Baggi game."* The object of the game was to learn how to endure pain. To that end we hit each other or stuck ourselves with sewing needles. At the same time we practised not showing that we were in pain, that is, not crying or shouting. It was also important, however, not to show where and when it hurt the most. For if I let it show when or where Father's blows really hurt, he remembered it and the next time hit precisely on those places. It was thus simplest to hide the pain when Father beat us.

Father was, after all, in Stalingrad. There, unexpectedly, the enemy had beaten him. After he came home from there, he beat Mama and us, especially when he was drunk. In addition, Father had vowed to be on guard and not let the enemy ever overrun him again. Therefore, when we were in school he searched our rooms. "Inspection" is what he called this procedure, which meant that he searched through every drawer, shelf, and cabinet, and even the beds for enemy material. Enemy material could be a piece of Western chewing gum, a glossy trading card, or a subway ticket from which one could learn that I had been on the Vineta Strasse subway line travelling towards the Stadtmitte (city centre) stop at 11:32 on Sunday morning.* When I then came home, the interrogation began. Where from Pankow* were you headed at 11:32 on Sunday morning? If I did not know, I was beaten. If I did know I was still beaten. Because he, Father, had not learned where I was roaming around. But then he never learned where I was, since I was constantly deceiving him. But we ought not to have taken him for a fool. He would soon get it out of us. Such victories of Father's over a subway ticket, a piece of gum, or a Western trading card encouraged me to practise hiding early on. Since Father also searched our rooms when we were present, I made a note of places in the wardrobe or under the windowsill. My hiding places would have to be more sophisticated. They could not be recognized as hiding places. With Father, thus, I practised playing hide and seek.

I held a grudge against my mother my entire life for not kicking my father out. I did not understand her argument that he was, after all, her husband and our father. What did that have to do with anything? Her protestations that she did not want to end up like her mother were not convincing either. Her mother, my Westoma, married someone new every seven years: because either she had chased the men away or they had died on her. My mother had no chance of becoming like her, if only because she was so unmusical. My grandmother was a singer, and as such she had enjoyed some success. My grandmother was particularly unhappy with my mother's marriage. She pitied my father, but that my mother destroyed her life with him was not love, she said, but incredible stubbornness.

Through my father, a son of the working class, my mother made a sort of amends on the part of the bourgeoisie to the exploited class. For in East Berlin, which she did not want to leave for any reason, she bore the stigma of not being a member of the working class but rather the bourgeois intelligentsia. She thus had to atone to Father for her sin and always had to do something extra for the first Workers' and Peasants' State in Germany,* even though her contributions to it were already praiseworthy. My mother had to serve the working class, as she said. Therefore, she was also in the SED. I was jealous of and angry at this Party in which my mother was a member and for which she soon worked as a functionary. That is to say: my mother and even my Ostopa never had time for me because they were always on the go promoting the happiness of all humanity. That was always more important to them than I was, and it hurt me. My Westopa, who in East Berlin was regarded as the enemy, had all kinds of time for me. Especially on Sundays, after he had come with me from church. Then he was especially cheerful and good-natured. For that I loved him.

I lived with the border, I lived on the border, I lived along the border. There were streets in Berlin where the left side belonged to the Eastern and the right side to the Western part of the city. The People's Police (Volkspolizei) in the East were not allowed on the right side of the street, because they would then have left the democratic sector of Berlin. The police on the West side had similar instructions, just from different authorities. Many kids did what I did: they played their little games with the policemen from both sides. They insulted them and then ran to the other side of the street, that is, to another part of the city, where a different occupying power was in control.

Since the policemen served as the police of two powers that were hostile towards each another, they could not help each other out while they were on duty.

Passing from one street to another and arriving in another world and thus entering another value system was fascinating for me. Suddenly other rules applied, which I made an effort to master so that I could move freely within both systems. I made a game out of crossing the border from one system to another. No one should be able to tell by looking at me whether I had just crossed from the West into the East, or was about in the West just after entering from the East. I wanted to remain unrecognized.

Over the years, East and West Berlin became two stages for me, each with different repertoires, props, and actors. And to a certain degree this was true, even from the perspective of lighting conditions, which are a part of any set design. When I was in West Berlin, the colourful advertising signs, of which I could never get enough, glowed. When I came to East Berlin, light was no longer a factor in the production. Instead, there were watchwords and maxims about freedom and socialism, and against imperialist warmongers everywhere. The stores were not called Bilke or Wertheim as in the West, but HO and Konsum.* When there was something to buy there, long lines formed in front of the shops.

Two playhouses with different programs: that made an impression on me. Pivotal to the stages were the currencies. Thus I was soon carrying two coin purses with me, one with East money, one with West money. I carried other symbols around with me in my school bag. Tennis socks for when I visited my Westoma at the Schlachtensee in the summer.* A lot of kids wore tennis socks and white shorts there. I changed clothes behind the bushes during the warmer months of the year and in the hallways during the winter, so that when I arrived at the place I had sought out, I looked like a native. When I travelled to East Berlin and had to wear my pleated skirt, I dug it out from the bottom of my gym bag and changed into my costume for the visit with my parents on the East Berlin stage.

Changing East and West just like changing rooms within an apartment, with a naturalness that was not worth mentioning since it was a part of everyday life, just like waking up and going to school – that is what I practised in my youth: moving easily from one system to another.

Changing systems as one changed rooms, where a different piece of music had to be played in another tonality, had developed early on my ability to think abstractly and nurtured my sense for contrapuntal intensifications and their potential resolutions. For that reason too I developed a precocious interest in counterpoint as a compositional principle and loved Bach's *The Art of Fugue*.

How I ever would have survived the cold and the hot war in Berlin without my piano, I do not know. But alongside my divided existence in the frontline city I invented another. It came out of my piano. Note by note I played out its melody. Or perhaps the piano played the notes to me? I do not know. I never knew. For by God and all the wars that had been fought in Berlin, I had these notes all the same. They had been born with me and rang out. My utmost concern was not to lose them. For, from the beginning, I had a premonition that if I ever lost the notes I would be lost. For a long time, though, I just could not articulate this. But I felt the anxiety when I did not hear the notes because Father was yelling so loud. Then I began to cry and begged him not to drown out my notes. When he did not stop, I closed all the doors behind me. I put my hands over my ears and with great concentration hummed my melody in ever new variations. I thought, the more variations that came to me, the more likely I would remember at least one of them. I hummed the notes and played them on the piano as long as it took until they vibrated clear and bright within me and I was certain that the war on the other side of the door could not touch them and me any more. Then I opened the door behind me again. Even if Father stood next to me, I no longer heard what he was shouting about. That is, I saw his mouth move, but I only heard the notes and the variations on them that I had invented.

My Westoma also heard these notes. She said that they were a gift from God. On no account was I to lose them, and she helped me to retrieve these notes from my piano. So I could keep my melody, she nourished my piano playing with lessons. Soon I learned how to play the piano everywhere, whether on the streetcar or during gym class. I practised my fingerings on the pavement and on window panes, on the desks at school or in Father's favourite bars. But was I playing or was the music playing within me? That too was something I could never say with certainty. Soon I was taking piano lessons at the conservatory in West Berlin. My grandmother financed my musical education, including lessons in ballet and movement, since, she said, those also were a part of an artist's training. Later I received instruction in ear training and composition and played in the West Berlin Conservatory's children's division.

As my second instrument at the conservatory, I learned to play the organ. Soon I was entirely lost to the earthly world and focused only on the notes, their melody and playing piano. I had blocked out the cold and the hot war and, with it, the world in which I lived. I had exchanged the border between East and West for the bounds of the ability to play ever more complicated piano pieces. With the mastery of these pieces, I opened up one door after another to a world where other rules applied. That their keys lay with me, with my ability to play a piece of music, delighted me. The better I played, the sooner I could cross new borders and access new rooms into which I allowed only whom and what I wished: Bach's and Mozart's piano sonatas; my grandmother and Schubert's *Winterreise*; my piano teacher and *The Well-Tempered Clavier;** Inge, the flutist; and Vivaldi. I barred the door to my father and every teacher who ran around shouting. It fascinated me that, through my piano, I had learned to block out the "world." For I not only learned how to open up doors, I also learned to close doors behind me. Now and then I drifted about the entire day with my notes and was astonished when I reappeared in the other world, where I was travelling on the S-Bahn to school or had to write a dictation, something on which I never could concentrate. Or when I sat in the kitchen at my parents' home and was already on my fifth jam sandwich, as my sister assured me convincingly. Sometimes I experienced difficulty switching from the world of sound to the East-West world. I did not always find my way into the latter soon enough. Occasionally I was afraid that I would not find my way back from the world of sound, was afraid that I could lose myself in sound that spread endlessly outward in concentric circles, carrying me along with each new outermost circle. When the fear turned into real anxiety, because I had been carried away too far from any sort of centre, it gave me the creeps to be so alone with the music. To make the anxiety go away in such situations, I began to sing and was overwhelmed by my voice, which at times sang alone over an entire orchestra.

And so, I had succeeded in forgetting the real world in which I went about. On top of the first, I had built a second world for myself.

My mother was also building another world that had nothing to do with mine. Hers was the socialist world, for which she worked tirelessly. Since the great battle of liberation for humanity claimed all of my mother's energies, there was not any time left over. Nevertheless, since we were still supposed to have order in our lives, my siblings and I were divided up among relatives. I had to understand it, my mother said, and she was truly sorry, but the struggle for the future of all humanity and its happiness simply had priority now. I did not understand. After all, I did not know humanity. But then no one ever asked me either. My older sister went to our Ostoma, and I to our Westoma. And I understood immediately that this was great news for me. So from 1953, with very few interruptions, I lived with my grandmother in West Berlin. There stood my piano, there I felt at home.

I had forgotten the Cold War. I was on course to becoming a pianist and deliberated with my teacher over what I should play for the main exam in piano at the conservatory, since I desperately wanted to be accepted for the master class. He explained to me why the Sonatas and Partitas of Bach were better for me than Mozart's Sonata in A Major (KV 331), which I could not get away from at the time. Then on 13 August 1961 the Cold War struck.

My mother had bought a summer house close to Berlin. It was the custom that I spend at least some of my summer vacation with my parents. My mother had the need to spend her few days of vacation with me too. After all, I was her daughter. I really did not understand the argument. But the sailboat, which I could use when I was at my parents' home, was enough of a temptation for me to spend two, even three weeks in East Germany.

Only later did I recall that it was precisely that August when my grandmother and mother got into a row over the question of rights and whose daughter I really was. It was never resolved, as usual, but my mother prevailed for the moment and, against my grandmother's will, decided that I would spend my vacation with her. At breakfast on 11 August, my grandmother again asked me if I really wanted to go, since the political situation was so tense. But I did not want to hear anything of the East-West games or politics. So on Sunday, 13 August, I was floating on a lake in East Germany and only learned a day later that the Wall stood.

For years I wondered whether my mother, who at that time had already made a small career for herself in the Stalinist party and worked in the propaganda division of the SED district committee office, had known about the Wall's imminent construction. I could never rid myself of the suspicion that she had lured me into the East with the promise of being allowed to use the sailboat for an entire weekend. Whenever I brought it up later, she reacted defensively. She had not known anything about the Wall's construction. Only her class instinct, as she put it, had told her that something was up. It would thus be better to retrieve me from West Berlin. For had I been "over there" when the Wall went up, my mother believed, it would have been disastrous for her future: having a daughter who had "fled" the Republic would have cost her her position. I was, after all, a first-degree relative; that would have sufficed. Thanks to her class instinct my mother secured her future: a modest career in the SED Party apparatus.

My future, however, was abruptly cut short. I did not immediately grasp what had happened. My grandmother sent telegrams and letters. She urged me not to go over the Wall. She would get me out. Since my grandmother was the only authority, apart from Bach, that I accepted, I believed her. I played further on a borrowed piano that soon stood in my parents' apartment, and prepared myself for the main exam in piano in the Eastern part of the city, which I could take at the conservatory in East Berlin.

The atmosphere at my parents' was unbearable. Whenever he came home, Father raged that I should cease my plonking about on the piano already. My playing also got on my siblings' nerves. My older sister solicited their sympathies, by trying to make it clear that I was not quite all there and thus needed to play. Thus, albeit in a friendly way, she echoed Father's opinion. She always had compassion for me.

In order to endure what was really an intolerable situation at my parents', I tried to block out everything that did not resonate. I concentrated right up to the breathing on the piece I was playing. I played the piece until I was resonating in it myself. I played myself into a trance. I successfully practised extending the period of time during which I resonated in a piece. In these trances I was soon spending the whole day, which I passed fully detached from myself. All I cared about was preventing the piece from stopping. In this way, I could withdraw myself from the life around me that was actually unbearable. While sitting and standing, while running and taking a walk, I was soon concentrating completely on my pieces, either in my thoughts or right at the piano.

As long as I played, nothing and no one could reach me. Only when the melody within me ceased and I could no longer find it on the piano did I start to panic. For the world that I refused to acknowledge suddenly stood right next to me and grinned at me. Then it became so loud around me that I felt as if I would suffocate instantly because I could not breathe for all the noise. Sometimes, during such states of panic, I still managed to cover my ears and sing my piece or invent my own. Then for hours I hummed it or played it on the piano. If Father came and shook me or boxed my ears because I refused to stop playing, and I did not feel his blows because of my playing, I knew that I had even beaten him out with my playing. Content, I then drifted on the notes, but where to I do not know. Wilfully I fought with the music against any sort of rhythmification until I had closed the distance between one note and another. I struck notes against notes contrapuntally and released them, ringing, from their sound space. My goal was for them not to return and ring out again in the spaces from which I had just retrieved them. Wilfully I ground the tones together until, in their unprotected sound state, they were drawn together in a way that had never been heard before. In this state of never heard sound I drifted on.

One day though I really went too far. I went past myself, went past all the tones and their sounding spaces. Unawares, one door after another slammed shut behind me. I was trapped and could no longer figure my way out. Now the doors only opened inwards, if at all. I was driven by fear. It forced me to scream and I was so alone with my fear that I lost consciousness.

When I came around, a friendly nurse was standing at my bed asking whether I wanted brown bread or crispbread for breakfast. Out of pure fear I started to cry. She gave me a shot of something to calm me. I fell back asleep. In the coming weeks, I learned how to stay calm to avoid receiving more shots. I acknowledged what the doctors explained to me: piano playing had made me sick and I had to give it up if I did not want to remain under psychiatric care forever. I did not understand, but neither did I hear my notes any more. My melody was gone.

Later I understood that I had fallen between the two worlds, East-West. There could be no more playing with them, I was stuck in the East.

2

My rather involuntary stay in the German Democratic Republic thus began with my gradual release from the psychiatric clinic ward.

At first there were hour-long walks in the clinic park. These were prescribed as practice sessions for my recovery. Trial releases followed, initially just over the weekend. That did not work out so well. For I did not know where to go. Going to my parents was not exactly enjoyable, particularly since Father had always known that I had never been normal, otherwise I would not have endured my own plonking on the piano. That I landed in the nut house was only logical, he declared, and the fault of my grandmother and mother alone. She should have taken the jangle box away from me, precisely because I had a screw loose from the start. But no one would listen to him. And why not? Because no one ever took him seriously. Because people simply thought that, as a son of the working class, he did not know what was going on. By "people" he meant my grandmother in particular, but also my mother. He felt that, as it affected me, they had certainly done enough damage. It was good that it had all now come to an end.

Over the years I had lost all emotional contact with my siblings; we had been socialized in entirely different worlds. There was little tying us together as siblings.

My mother tried to be nice to me. But it was embarrassing to her that I had been under psychiatric care. She tried to cover up my situation among our relatives as much as possible. Clinic, yes, but not a psychiatric one, she made me understand. Not everyone needed to know that, right?

The second phase of my gradual release from the clinic meant that I only had to return to the hospital for the night to sleep. That was already better. During this time, my mother provided me with generous amounts of money. She wanted me to come back home. She truly wanted this, I believe. But I was dead set against it. I still put a good portion of the blame on her for being stuck in the East, liberated from the class enemy. I also made her mostly to blame for having ruined my musical existence. Later I despised her for never having left Father, whom she had let humiliate her, even allowing herself to be beaten.

I never had much desire to try to think too much about the possible reasons for my mother's decisions. They were certainly also connected with my grandmother. My grandmother had a strong personality: charm, cleverness, and charisma were inseparable parts of her. As a singer, she was certainly disappointed with her only daughter, because she was so astonishingly unmusical. Certainly my mother suffered from this, just as she had suffered from the fact that, precisely because of my musicality, my grandmother now loved me above everything instead of her and thanked God, as she put, that in me she finally got a daughter after all. I could never be forgiving towards my mother. After all, neither my siblings nor I had asked to be brought into the world.

After my definitive release from the mental hospital, I did not return to my parents. My personal possessions fitted into a travel bag that I pulled through the streets of my compulsorily prescribed homeland. Of course, I was registered with the police somewhere in Berlin. Not to have a fixed abode was a punishable offence. But to register somewhere using a friend's address and sticking a name plate on their mailbox was just a formality.

Someone or other advised me to go for vocational counselling, since being unemployed was also illegal. It was called being asocial.* A counsellor at the career centre strongly suggested that I learn a respectable trade, before I even considered the idea of attending university. A seamstress, for example; there were apprenticeships available for that. When I asked what that entailed, I was told that I would learn how to sew bed linens in this trade. The joy in my face must not have been very great. Therefore the counsellor suggested that I become a gardener: that was said to be good for the nerves. Or a precision mechanic: with my prior history as a pianist I had good qualifications for that too. He advised me to mull it over. I did so and never returned to the career centre again.

I made do for myself with odd jobs. I did not need very much at the time. I did not have any goal worth living for. Why I was even still alive and walking about, I did not understand myself. Only slowly did I hit upon the idea of ending my life. I was speechless after the collapse of my musical world. I had not learned how to express myself in a language other than that of music. Moreover, all the other forms of expression seemed, if not inferior, then at least unusable, for me at any rate. I did not know how to talk about what had happened. What I said was awkward and crude. The words did not express what I wanted to say. I became afraid to speak because my alienation confronted me, unmistakable and undisguised.

I liked best to work silently on the night shift at the state-owned Narva light bulb factory.* This work had nothing to do with me personally and was well paid. The workers tolerated me, despite my constant absent-minded expression, because I did my job.

At the time, I had an almost uncontrollable urge to steal. If I were forced to live in the first German Workers' and Peasants' State, then I also wanted to have something from it. After all, the property belonged to everyone. So I took what I needed to live from the people's property.

For almost two years I schlepped my bag through Berlin-Brandenburg.* Meanwhile, I had met Deddi, Maria, and Leisten-Paul. Before 1961, Deddi had been a so-called "cross-border commuter." He lived in the East and worked in the West. His wages were also split, fifty per cent in the West, fifty per cent in the East. Before the Wall went up, Deddi did well for himself financially. In West Berlin, he worked as a purchaser for a hotel. Now and again he told of how he smuggled eggs, butter, and meat from the East to the West and how all the participants in the operation benefited. That he got stuck in the East after 13 August 1961 was something that he never came to terms with. Deddi owned a truck; he also had tremendous anger towards the GDR. This anger over being locked up united us. Facing the future,* which ended in front of the Wall, we soon agreed that we had to do something to deal with our socialist luck. Motivated by this anger, we organized the theft of wooden fencing.

I had met Deddi through Maria. Maria also worked at the light bulb factory. More and more we arranged to work the night shift together. She had debts to pay off, as she later told me. Maria was impressed with my sense of hearing. I could tell her, for instance, when the conveyor belt on which we sorted the light bulbs would stall. I heard it beforehand, since the rotational speed of the motor driving the belt became irregular just before it broke down. I told her then that we could soon go and smoke a cigarette. During these smoking and gossip breaks we became friends. We also drew the regular rate for the night, even if the belt was not running due to a mechanical problem.

Once I had become better acquainted with Maria, I told her about the headaches that I frequently got from the noise in the machine room. One day she asked me if I would be willing to be on guard as a listener while they stole fencing material. That would be good for everyone. They had almost been caught once already because no one had heard the approach of someone out for a stroll. Of course, I would not only have to listen carefully, but also drag out fencing. I agreed and during the entire winter dragged the wood for snow fences from the people's own fields with Maria and Deddi. Leisten-Paul had a private shop for garden equipment. He stained the wood a dark-brown colour in his sheds so that it looked like regular fencing material and then sold it on the sly. As with everything else, materials for garden fences were in short supply in the GDR. And the number of garden plot owners was increasing just then. One could get by on the earnings made by selling snow fencing. So I switched from the night shift in the light bulb factory to the night shift with Deddi. I also took my work with him more seriously than I had my job at the people's own factory because now my earnings depended, to a large degree, on me, my cleverness, and my ideas.

As winter came to an end so, too, did our seasonal work. The farmers on the collective farms gathered up what was left of the snow fencing in the fields. Deddi and Maria moved with their truck towards the Baltic. I had saved some money and squatted in an empty apartment. It was rather run down, but cozy. At the time I lived very spartanly. I stole only what I needed to eat – and books, especially the classics: Hölderlin, Schiller, Kleist, Büchner, and Eichendorff.* It was the first time since I had left my grandmother's that I again spent time reading. Even as a fifteen-year-old, Hölderlin had been my favourite poet, and so he remained for decades to come.

During this period, Aufbau Press published a really good series of classics. I soon possessed a complete set. Someone or other had given me a volume of Rilke as a present. I read poetry and plays like an addict. During the summer, however, my savings from the people's property ran out. That was at a time when meat was again being rationed in Berlin. In order to receive meat, you had to choose a particular butcher's shop by having it take down your address. As much as I was addicted to poetry during that summer, I developed a real hankering for meat as autumn arrived. While I was still playing piano, I always ate steaks during the exam periods. My grandmother swore by steaks as a means to combat the stress of exams; consequently, I thus also believed in the invigorating effect of beef steaks.

Whether there was first a shortage of meat and then my hunger came or the other way around, I cannot say with certainty. In any case, the allotment of two pounds of meat per week, give or take, was not enough for the hunger that had so suddenly overcome me. A sign in a private butcher's shop – Sales Assistant Wanted – gave me an idea: I could be rid of my hunger here. I went into the store and announced that I wanted to work as a sales assistant. The master butcher looked me over from head to toe and then back to the head. I was very thin at the time. I believe that for a moment the butcher was not at all sure that I was not pulling his leg. I repeated my offer with all the seriousness I could muster. He then inspected my hands. He wanted to test my grip. I said nothing about having been a pianist. I grasped his hand firmly. He gave me the job. He showed me the hand positions to use so that I did not cut my finger when slicing roulades.* He showed me how to manage a cleaver and bones, and how to handle a sausage knife. Then he left me alone. He never even once harassed me sexually. I was too thin for him, was what he said. And for that reason too, he let me eat as much meat and sausage as I wanted. Of course, only during work hours. And for the weekend he always gave the other sales assistants and me something fine "for the Sunday roast," as he put it.

It was thus as a sales girl in a private butcher's shop that I had my first proper job in the Workers' and Peasants' State.

After I had, in fact, regained my strength through beef roasts and cutlets, the winter season and my work in the butcher's so got on my nerves that I became depressed. "100 g of Jagdwurst, 100 g of liverwurst, and a 150 g piece of Thüringer"* – "We don't have any beef tenderloin," while thinking: not for you anyway. "But we do have smoked pork ribs which are very nice. Ask again though on Friday. We get new supplies then. Perhaps there will be something there ..." The daily monotony. Always the same grips and conversations, the same customers and sales assistants' comments. What does that have to do with me? That can't be a life, not for me anyway.

But I refused to come to terms with the circumstances in which I was living. I went about as if I had thrown a blanket over myself that made me invisible even to myself. I had fallen into a sort of twilight state with no interest in the GDR, politics, or socialist nonsense. I did not even read the newspaper at the time, since the East German newspaper-speak made me nauseous.

My own emptiness made me very fearful. One day this fear prompted me to take all the pills that the psychiatrists had prescribed to me over several months, but that I had not taken – only hoarded. I woke up in a hospital. The ward where I lay was called the resuscitation ward. My bed was surrounded by blue oxygen tanks. I felt wretched and was furious at the doctors and nurses who were fighting for my life, as they put it. What was my life to them? I wanted to end it and they had no right to interfere.

When I was released from the clinic, I again did not have a place to stay. Strolling through the hospital, however, I had read the notice: "Nurses and nurses' assistants wanted. Possibility of lodging in the nurses' dormitory." I went to the personnel department and applied. Two days later I began as an assistant in a surgery ward. I brought in and took away meal trays, learned to set up beds and disinfect bedpans. Soon I had learned everything that was to be learned as a nurse's assistant.

The emptiness in my head and the fear returned. I tried a second time to kill myself. When I woke up in the resuscitation ward and saw the same doctors and nurses who had brought me back "to life," I swore to myself on the blue oxygen tanks by my bed not to land here again. Not only because even here in the medical sequence of resuscitation measures I feared the routine. I also understood, even if only vaguely, that I really did not want to die. For the first time, the question about the meaning of all life and existence arose in me with great intensity. With tremendous zeal I reflected on their WHAT, WHY, and WHEREFORE in order to get answers to these questions.

I moved in with Alex. I had met him at a late-night bar. Now and then I frequented the place when I could not sleep because my vague night fears had become so strong.

Alex dreamed of motorcycles, cars, of high-end record players and modern radios. Alex thought in very concrete terms and was always tinkering with some sort of motor or radio. He was an electrical engineer. My abstract and lyrical questions about the meaning of life did not mean a thing to him. He loved the forest, not Eichendorff's poems about the forest. We went camping together a lot and went sailing. He got me into his sailing club, which he could use as a member of his company trade union. Alex took me back to nature: we gathered and dried mushrooms, picked berries, and made jam. We canned and preserved food for the winter. When I asked him for which winter – since we were already dead in the middle of it – he looked at me blankly. Alex was good to me. I lacked the strength then for a great love. But it reassured me that I was no longer alone – even at night when the fear awoke and

I was carried away on its cry – for at such moments I could hold tight to Alex and feel his breath.

During this period my mother paid attention to me again. It grieved her that I had tried to kill myself. After all, she said, she did love me. It also made her uncomfortable, since, ultimately, it was her daughter who refused to see that the socialist fatherland offered her, just like everyone else, an enormous opportunity if only she wanted to seize it …

There was no provision for suicide attempts within the socialist program's ideology for happiness; they were morally unjustifiable. After all, the future belonged to socialism and thus to me too. It was entirely my fault that I could not appreciate how lucky I was to be able to take part in a brighter future for humanity. I was being stubborn, my mother insisted. I wanted to hurt her; that was the deeper reason for my acts of defiance. When I tried to make it clear to her that my socialist life here had got on my nerves, that routine work was wearing me out, and that I was dying from the monotony, she promised to try to find me work in which I could find fulfilment, as she put it. And, in fact, she did see to it: I was hired as a cultural functionary in a large hospital complex.

My mother pulled strings through the borough's SED district committee office to set it up. She herself acted as the guarantor for my political reliability and spoke of the great confidence she had placed in me for this position and of the great risk she had taken in doing so. Therefore, I was not to disappoint her. Of course, only much later did I comprehend that a principle of family inheritance was being applied here: my mother's political reliability was being transferred to me, without my actual suitability for the job ever having been taken into consideration.

The only requirement that I had to fulfil for this placement was largely a formality: namely, to join the Federation of Free German Trade Unions (the Freier Deutscher Gewerkschaftsbund or FDGB). I discussed joining the union with Alex. He did not think I needed to worry about joining the FDGB. He himself was a member, but mainly on account of its sailing club. In addition, one had access to low-cost vacations through the union. He thus saw no problems with me joining. I wouldn't lose anything by doing it. I therefore joined the union and suddenly became a cultural functionary in a large hospital. I was supposed to organize socialist cultural programs for doctors and nurses. But what did I know about that? I fell back on what I did know. For my first event, I organized a concert of the doctors' orchestra for the eve of May First: Handel, Bartok, Brahms.* I got on well with the doctors and the questions we received were primarily about music. Alongside concerts, I organized dance performances. I also programmed public readings, which were prepared together with the staff at the union's library.

The program notices for the weekly organ vespers at the local church gave me the idea of asking the pastor if we might hold a series of baroque organ concerts there. He was very taken with the idea. I had no inkling that I was not supposed to make common cause with the church. The first concert took place on a Friday. The organist played Bach and Buxtehude and the church was jam-packed. Two days later, when the organist fell sick and could not play for the service, the pastor rang the doorbell to our place at the crack of dawn. He asked whether, exceptionally, I might play the organ. I had told him that the organ was my secondary instrument at the conservatory. Half asleep as I was, I could only say yes. He waited until I had got dressed, then we drove to the church in his Trabant.* Even though I was still fighting my morning drowsiness, I remember clearly that I first played Bach's organ arrangement of the chorale "Wachet auf, ruft uns die Stimme" (Awake, a voice is calling).

The following day I was summoned to the office of the hospital's medical director. In his office, the chairman of the trade union; the secretary of the state youth organization, the Free German Youth (the Freie Deutsche Jugend or FDJ); and the Party secretary for the hospital were all waiting for me. I was greeted with the question: Which voices were supposed to awaken in the church? Did I not know that, especially these days, the enemy sits in the church pews? When I started to explain myself by saying that I did not encounter any enemy at that hour of the morning and that, moreover, the chorale had been written more than two hundred years ago and was thus no ideological fight song, the Party secretary interrupted me: It was scandalous that I had played for a church service. I was a trade union functionary here, which apparently I had not understood so far. Was I not in my right mind politically? I was not, in fact, which is why I didn't understand the grounds for all the commotion. When I asked where I should play the organ, since ultimately there were organs only in churches and not in union meeting halls, the director of the hospital went berserk. He spoke of a political provocation without parallel. When I tried to explain that, as far as I knew, Bach didn't give a damn about politics, the director sent me from the room. I was fired from the position I had just obtained.

For the time being, I was again out of work, although I was still a member of the Federation of Free German Trade Unions. Alex consoled me by saying that such a membership could lie dormant and that I would still get the trade union discount for the FDGB trip he had put in for. And even as an inactive member, I could still use the sailing club. These were the factual comments of an electrical engineer, something I really liked about Alex.

3

I lost once more my desire for regular employment. I withdrew and worked part-time at the light bulb factory. As long as no special expenses, such as vacation or a winter coat, were pending, two night shifts each week were enough. Living in East Germany was inexpensive, if one disregarded all middle-class distinctions of taste. And anyway I had long ago rejected as rubbish the middle-class standards tied to eating, drinking, living conditions, and dress. I had degraded eating to the mere intake of food, sticking to the so-called "basic foods" as the East German officials so aptly called them. These basic foods were available for practically nothing; housing too. Rents had little more than symbolic value. A newly built apartment with a bath, warm water, and central heating was coveted by families with children. That these apartments were built in the Lego-block system of prefabricated housing* was mocked, if at all, only by intellectuals and then mainly because of the buildings' uniformity.

This experience, that you could eat, drink, and live basically for free if you ignored everything else, counted among my most important experiences in East Germany. In the simplest sense of the word, no one could die of hunger in the GDR, not even in protest. You could eat or live poorly, but if someone wanted to sleep on a park bench or in some train station even, the police would pick him up and place him in a police shelter.

That men do not live on bread alone is something that people knew even before Brecht.* In addition to shelter, a part of what man also needed flashed by the East Germans every night on the screen during the commercial breaks on West German television. In black and white at first, later in colour. I trained myself at the time to have little need of everyday things. Instead, just like many other intellectuals in the East German "Republic of Reading," I consumed books.

I balanced out my spartan lifestyle by consuming philosophical texts. I eagerly devoured one book after another: Heidegger, Nietzsche, and Sartre. Before the Wall went up, Alex's sister had been buying these philosophical texts regularly. I first read Heidegger's *Holzwege* (*Off the Beaten Track*) as if spellbound and was excited by each new sentence that I conquered. I did not understand much of what I read. But I was struck by the rhythm of Heidegger's language. And with each sentence he hit me anew, dealt me a blow, and instilled fear in me. Indeed, it was the panic that had been bottled up, and the despair, which found no other way out of me except for self-destruction. In Heidegger there was already a linguistic expression of just this kind of existential panic. So, my crazy fear also had a location outside of me. It could be communicated. In this respect, Heidegger's theories also calmed me, even when they drove me ever deeper into despair. To express what had happened and bridge my own emptiness with language was the intention I could only express once I had found language again.

Alex liked my reflectiveness, to which he had no access. It made me resemble his older sister, whom he loved more than anything. Alex felt himself drawn in strange ways to metaphysical questions; until he met me, though, he had been able to keep his distance from them. In part this was because his sister also kept a certain distance from her younger brother, something I was not at all capable of managing.

Alongside Heidegger, I read Hölderlin's *Hyperion*. I read him every day, like a Bible. The mourning for something that was irretrievably lost, of which each page of his book spoke, brought me the certainty that I was not alone with loss. Rather by chance, at this time I also picked up a paperback copy of Hegel's *Phenomenology of Spirit* that I found at Alex's sister's. It was the first book of Hegel's that I read. The rhythm with which Hegel wrote was familiar to me, the melody of his sentences recognizable. They reminded me of Bach; more specifically, of the structure of a Bach fugue, of the sequence of steps for linking one note to another and of how the omission of one single step threatened to cause the entire composition to collapse. Indeed, reading Hegel's sentences reminded me of *The Art of Fugue*. At long last, something had reappeared that was familiar to me from my now shattered musical existence: a rhythm, a sound that I desperately wanted to hold on to. I was overflowing with life experiences, to which I could add that of my personal collapse; indeed I had to add that in, for at some point I had to be done with what I had experienced so that I could go on living. If the extent of the rupture could be calculated, there was a chance that I would not fall again through the cracks into an abyss. If there were rules for continuity, then there were also rules that made its stoppage calculable.

So, at last, I had found a frequency at which communication could be attempted, an understanding that would perhaps manage to remove my lack of language. Far away from the real world in which I lived, I heard a wavelength that to me seemed appropriate for communication. I set the rhythm of Heidegger's sentences against that of Hegel. That, for Hegel, a rupture was not a caesura, as it was in Heidegger, again and again caused me to prick up my ears. It was a sort of trance into which these sentences could transport me. Far from the hustle and bustle of daily life, I went to my night shifts in the light bulb factory, packed the bulbs in their blue cardboard boxes, and was preoccupied with Hegel's notions of being and nothing.

I had found for myself a manageable balance between work on the production line and existential philosophy, and things inside me were pretty much on the right track, when Alex's sister approached me. She thought that I had probably recovered enough energy by now and should take a chance at learning a proper trade. She had made inquiries at the technical school for medical careers at the hospital where she worked as a medical assistant. There were still openings that year for students wishing to pursue careers as dieticians. I should apply. Since Alex shared his sister's opinion, I took a look at what this might entail. I received a demonstration of the dietician's job in one of the school's training kitchens. In countless small pots, meals were being prepared for people with liver disorders, as were gall bladder diets, broth for dyspeptics, and bland meals for renal patients. Female students in white hairnets went around tasting their soups.

The idea that, from September on, I would also be standing in front of such small pots and stirring low-salt meals mobilized life forces that had, in fact, come back to me. I energetically dealt with being admitted to university to study philosophy. Alex was not very keen on that. He wanted me to learn a proper trade. For him, "proper" was what his sister did, if I did not want to study engineering as he had. He had found out about my mathematical inclinations long ago.

I stuck with philosophy. Alex's sister understood me and helped. She knew someone in Leipzig who knew someone in Leipzig who, in turn, knew the dean of the Faculty of Arts and Humanities. I told this very dean the sad story of the demise of my musical existence. Since he himself was interested in music and had a sister whose whole life revolved around music, as he put it, he had some understanding for musical talent. For a long time we sat together in a *Speisegaststätte*, as restaurants were called in the GDR. He listened patiently to what I had to say about language and music. Over Sauerbraten with Thuringian dumplings and red cabbage I explained at length my ideas about the connection between Bach's counterpoint and Hegel's linguistic rhythm. I attempted to convince him that structural commonalities existed between them, which I sensed but was incapable of putting into words, which would of course change as soon as I had studied philosophy. A connection existed; I heard it quite clearly. He said that he could well believe me. And as far as Bach went, he believed me there too. What he could not believe, he later confessed to me, was that I did not know what philosophy in a socialist country was all about.

For the moment, though, he promised to look into things for me. He intimated that he knew something about the enrolment problems facing students who, like me, had stumbled. In the meantime, he noted, I should at least look at a textbook of Marxist-Leninist philosophy. I later received my offer of admission from him personally and went to Leipzig.

I owe it to the political authority vested in particular individuals and the possibility of its arbitrary use that, even coming through the back door, I eventually ended up where I actually wanted to be. Ultimately someone with the appropriate authority had intervened personally on my behalf and taken on the political responsibility for my actions. Within the political ruling class there were again and again people who stood up for me and took risks, because they had to reckon with the fact that I did not conduct myself in a politically correct fashion since I did not know what "politically correct" meant in East Germany. At the time, I took the civil courage of these members of the leadership cadre to be the humane actions of noble communists. That I was also politically disenfranchised was something I grasped only much later.

In the introductory lecture for Marxist-Leninst philosophy, I learned from a blond-haired and blue-eyed professor with a fat neck that no one could graduate from here who had not become a member of the SED and who would not act responsibly vis-à-vis the Workers' and Peasants' State. It took everything I had not to have a panic attack right there.

He spoke about the working class, which it was my highest duty to serve as a philosopher. I swallowed hard, since my father, from this working class, had just contacted the university. He had heard from my mother that I had left to study in Leipzig. He had called the university administration. He wanted to make clear, first, that I was not normal – one could ask any of the psychiatrists in Berlin about that – and, second, that I was a zero politically and morally. He also explained to the dean that he did not see at all why he should have to pay for my education. He did not dream of it. After all, he had not been able to go to college either. The dean explained to me that my parents had to pay and that I could take them to court. Parents who earned over a certain amount of money had to pay for their children's education. There were laws that covered these matters, and, he added, the university would support me. I could learn about the details at the vice chancellor for student affairs' office.

I did not have the strength or the courage for such a lawsuit. I decided to continue working the night shift in Leipzig. Not in a big factory, but rather at Leipzig Interhotel's late-night bar,* where I interviewed to be a barmaid. During a trial shift, my knowledge of wine and brandy, including knowing what kind of glass to use for which drink, convinced the bar staff. So it worked to my benefit here that I frequently had to help the servants set the table for the soirées at my grandmother's house. Since it was an Interhotel, most of the spirits were imported, that is, from the West. As for the wines, I had to learn that there was also wine from Hungary, Bulgaria, and Romania.

So, once again I had my program of contrasts. By day I heard lectures about the advantages of dialectical materialism and about how socialism would triumph. By night, I mixed cocktails and flirted in the Hotel Deutschland with the enemy who brought foreign currency. I also learned how to make functional use of my silence. I said nothing when I came bleary-eyed from the coloured-light bar* into my lecture on socialist theory and heard that under socialism there was no such thing as alienated work. For the first time since the collapse of my musical talent, I again had an objective. I wanted to know what the meaning of life and the world was.

I made the decision then never to bear children. I wanted to be able to stop my time at any time. In the event that I could not go on, I wanted to be able to depart from this life without leaving behind any responsibility to which I would have to answer. I had separated myself from my family. That is how I wanted to leave it.

The family I was making my way towards was large and indeterminate, my responsibility to it effectively without consequence. I was on my way to the philosophers of the Western World.

In Leipzig there was an excellent visiting professor from the Czechoslovakian Socialist Republic, who lectured on logic. That fascinated me: to attribute a value to what had been experienced. That meant finding a measure for experience and for what had been experienced. At first I buried myself in propositional logic until I was up to my head, then later in the logic of contradiction. Soon the magic words that got me through the day were "dialectical logic." Dialectics is the logic of contradictions. It was brilliant, taking "true" and "false" as one value. Elevating rupture to a principle. What a measure! Naming the contradictions and being able to bring them together logically. Forcing them into a particular order so that they became controllable.

I had at last found a timeless space where I could establish myself and which I could secure against that reality in which I had not been able to find my bearings. I was ready to go down the path of rational philosophy. I was picking up a thread, one that just had to go somewhere.

I was fascinated by the method, which I found really congenial emotionally. It was named the dialectical method: "Everything is, everything is not. Everything is, in that it is not. Being and nothing become something. What I set down, I raise – by setting it down – up again." What a dynamic! What a sound! These were also dance steps: what I put down with one step, I lifted again in the next step and still moved ahead. Thus, everything could also be different from what I had previously assumed. The answers, which I had before, could also be questions. If that were the case, then perhaps there was something wrong about even my fear and its magnitude. I had searched for such an uncertainty principle. It was wide enough for my experiences to find a place in it.

The "remainder" of my studies I shunted to the outer tracks. In other words, with respect to their contents, I tried not to let the entire unpleasantness come near me. I wasn't successful at first. I became sick from my first attempt to divide my person into essential and unessential parts. Soon I could not work at my coloured-light bar any more. The students from my year collected money so that I could make ends meet. It was well intentioned, but unbearable for me. I gave up my studies and returned to Berlin.

In his sober fashion, Alex offered his commentary: See, I told you, studying philosophy is complete nonsense and makes one sick. I didn't argue. I was happy when Alex brought me a warm bowl of soup. It took some time until I had recovered from myself and applied to be a secretary at an elementary school. The work itself was not especially difficult, but required a lot of concentration. I could not manage that. I was too preoccupied with being and nothing, which under certain conditions could be the same thing. I made unforgivable mistakes at work. After I had sent invitations for some event to the dairy that were supposed to go to the parents' council and sent the bills for the school's milk to the parents, the school director raised quite a ruckus. He wanted to have me transferred to the borough council's offices, where I could be a clerk. I could do less damage there, he said, for he would not tolerate me at his school any longer. I resigned and returned to the night shift at the light bulb factory. With that job, I could at least keep my head clear.

But it was rather evident that, while sorting and packing the light bulbs on the assembly line, I was not getting far with my questions about being and nothing and their intonation. Soon the words themselves circled in my head and, for a while, took on the cadence of the assembly line on which the light bulbs approached me.

I realized that I would have to start from the beginning once again. After some hesitation, I finally addressed the political premises behind the study of philosophy in the GDR so that this time I could manage my energies more wisely and efficiently.

I went to the Humboldt University, arranged for my matriculation to be transferred from Leipzig to Berlin, and in 1966 began again in the first year. First, though, I had to settle the tuition problem. It was pointless to deal with my parents. I found a solution in the very regulations on fees and scholarships. Namely, these stated that if I were married I could receive a scholarship regardless of what my parents earned. I therefore married my gay friend Dieter. Having the status of "married" was also convenient for him, because being gay then was still illegal in East Germany and was not just persecuted politically.* So, for an administrative fee of ten marks Dieter and I got married. We insisted on having a hyphenated last name. After the formal ceremony we both signed a private document in which we committed ourselves to filing for divorce one year later. The reason: sexual incompatibility. That is just what we did, without providing the high court with any of the details. The divorce cost 200 marks. Moreover, as a divorcée I was guaranteed a basic stipend of 185 marks a month. It was not much, but was enough to survive on.

Afterward Alex and I got married, although Alex still did not agree with my study of philosophy.

4

The academic year in Berlin began with the call-up to military preparedness training, which took place in Brandenburg.* This was cynically called "civilian defence." Since my student records indicated that I had worked as a nurse's assistant, I was deployed as a medic – without anyone consulting me first. In a grey uniform and with a Red Cross band on my arm I marched in lock step on Brandenburg's sandy ground. Left, two, three, four, Left, two, three ... I was quite appalled, but it made no sense to protest openly. I would have been expelled from the university on the spot. I decided to concentrate on my nursing knowledge and then pulled my personal emergency brake. I faked a fainting spell and was taken to the infirmary. Since I had had really low blood pressure all my life and every doctor became alarmed after measuring it, a medically plausible explanation beyond all political considerations was soon found for my condition. After the third fainting spell in the training camp I was declared unfit for civilian defence, transferred to my personal doctor, and brought back to Berlin in an ambulance.

Alex was scared stiff. Two Red Cross assistants had brought me to the apartment door. When they had left, I clapped my hands together and joyfully began to sing: "Unfit for duty, unfit for duty, do you understand?" Alex stood pale and speechless in the hall. He did not understand at all.

That was also something left over from my life with the piano: the ability to switch gears abruptly, which I had had to learn in order to go from one piano piece to another during a concert. To focus on a new piece, from one minute to another, in order to play it with the highest intensity. These sudden transformations, as Alex called them, upset him deeply. I did not understand at the time why he feared them and could not accept my ability as something positive. I naïvely attributed his lack of understanding to his deficient artistic sense. Here his dry objectivity, which I otherwise really appreciated, stood in the way. I did not suspect that my leaps between worlds could become threatening to him.

In terms of its social composition, the cohort that I joined was unusual even for those choosing to study philosophy. Never again was there such a high concentration of children from prominent families in one class. That is, over a third of all the students came from the East German establishment. They were the children of old communists or "antifascist resistance fighters," as the GDR's official political speak put it in order to avoid having to say "fighters against National Socialism," which bore too close a resemblance to "fighters against socialism." These old communists had been members of the German Communist Party (KPD). With Hitler's rise to power, most of them had emigrated from Germany, but some had survived the concentration camps. The old communists enjoyed particular respect and privileges in East Germany and made up the majority of the East German nomenklatura's leadership ranks.* Until I again encountered Esther, a friend from my early childhood and elementary school years among these children of the antifascists, I did not even know that such antifa-kids – as they gladly called themselves – even existed. Esther was glad at first, but was then irritated by our reunion at the university. She thought that I would be travelling around the world as a pianist after I had disappeared at my grandmother's in West Berlin, as she put it. The lecturers handled my classmate Esther with great care and respect. Her father was a major general in the East German People's Police (Volkspolizei), although that meant nothing to me.

I told her about my history with the Berlin Wall and my piano playing. Suddenly, Esther felt responsible for me. She saw that I understood very little politically and, from that moment forward, she helped me as she could. And, because of her father's position, Esther could help a lot. She would not permit someone to be unhappy in her socialist world.

Esther was born a few kilometres from Moscow and was raised by a Russian nanny. Her parents fought as partisans in the Red Army and after the war ended they worked as political officers in the re-education centres for German prisoners of war. When Esther came to Germany, she was five years old and spoke Russian as well as she did German. Esther had never been in West Berlin or West Germany. She was proud of that. She was deeply convinced of the correctness of East Germany's policies. Above all, she loved her father, whose political convictions she shared fully and completely.

Soon she invited me to come home with her. She said that her father would be glad to see me again. He had heard me play the piano at a school function when we were in the third grade, she said, and had not forgotten it.

Esther's home lay in Berlin-Pankow in an area heavily guarded by the police and other security forces. This was where all the leaders of the first Workers' and Peasants' State lived before Wandlitz was built.* Esther's family lived in a medium-sized house there, from which her father came to greet me when I arrived for the first time. He was wearing a highly decorated uniform of the German People's Police. I winced. He approached me and was extremely friendly to me, almost tender even, which irritated me. To me, policemen were bloody cops and nothing more. And Esther's father, Jonas, was a cop, even if he also had a sense of humour. In fact, Jonas did not fit into the picture I had of an East German big shot who lived in a house guarded by sentries. When I got ready to take my leave and asked him to sign my pass so that I could depart the secured area, he told me I could come to him whenever I was in distress or got panicky, even at night. He did not sleep much anyway. He also said he would put me on the guards' list of regular visitors. And he did that too.

I returned there again, even if Esther's mother could not stand me. But then she could not stand anyone whose parents had not been in the antifascist resistance. I disliked her just as much. She also scorned me, because, as she phrased it, my level of political consciousness was so low that it couldn't be taken seriously. Esther and Jonas always defended me before her. I also accepted Jonas's offer of protection. For me, Jonas became the noble communist. The exception that proved the rule. Soon I loved him like a father who protected me. And in fact, without his political power, which owing to his military rank was also personal, I would never have survived my studies at Humboldt University's Institute for Philosophy.

I thus lived the paradoxes that, more and more, were fascinating me philosophically. I felt secure under Jonas's protection, who, in his capacity as a major general in the German People's Police, contributed significantly to my being stuck in this country without any means of escape.

I felt safe in his house, which was guarded from the People, whom he was expected to protect as the People's chief policemen. Little town or "Städtchen" was what the functionaries who settled there affectionately called this place under military protection. I felt safe in the house of a Party functionary, who essentially made sure that I did not make it alive over the antifascist protective wall, as he called the Berlin Wall, always with pride in his voice. He told me that I was quite fortunate not to have left East Germany. I separated Jonas the person, to whom my affection belonged, from Jonas the political official.

To move contrary to what was expected became my strategy for surviving in the GDR. For a long time I was not able to name it, but that did not alter my modus operandi in the least. Against all common sense, I did not study botany but rather philosophy in order to emigrate from East German "reality" into the German forest. I searched for new meaning for my life and tried to flee from the actual reality of socialism into the central factory for East German apologetics, of all places. And contrary to expectations, I did manage to escape. For even before I became aware of it, I had plunged into the dialectical method and its logic. For that is what it was all about, at least for me. I searched for a logic for what I had experienced, in which all the contradictions found their place and coexisted with one another. I was driven into the philosophy of contradictions by this existential longing for harmony via theory, so Hegel was only a step away for me. Going from his *Wissenschaft der Logik* (*Science of Logic*) back to East German reality was laborious, and virtually impossible, if one just arranged it properly. So, I trained myself in pure theory right in the middle of the Marxist-Leninist school for political philosophy.

To live contrary to what was expected. To act contrary to the usual. To hide oneself so that the hideout is not recognizable as a hideout, so that it cannot be detected as a hideout. To conceal oneself in the full light of day! It was a chance to survive. It was congenial to me. In my childhood, I had practised playing hide and seek with Father. To live in at least two places at the same time. On the East-West carousel of the Berlin S-Bahn Ring I had begun to cultivate this condition. Had learned to fight the feeling of dizziness in transitioning from one state to another and then finding an equilibrium between the two states. And as a musician, which I always remained, part of the basics of playing was being able to handle two themes at once.

So, to practise the indispensable transitions without touching reality. This became the standard I strove to attain for my degree in philosophy. Only, I could not articulate it so then.

For the time being, I went to the children of the old communists, the children of the antifascists, who, I soon discovered, were largely of

Jewish descent. They talked a lot about the heroic struggle of their parents and stuck together in a way that left me on the outside, although I was there in their midst. They tolerated me in their circle because I was Esther's friend. In the evenings the children of the antifascists often sang partisan songs or songs from the workers' class struggle to a guitar. At some point really late in the evening, they sang Jewish songs like "Es brennt Brüder, es brennt" (It Burns, Brothers, It Burns); "Sag nie, du gehst den allerletzten Weg" (Never Say, You Are Taking the Very Last Road), or "Auf dem Wagen liegt ein Kälbchen" (On the Wagon Lies a Calf/Donna Donna).*

Towards the end of the evening, the Jewish children of the old communists sang, of all things, ghetto songs – although, for a long time, I did not know that they were ghetto songs. For until I ended up in the university that year, I knew virtually nothing about Jewish children living in East Germany. But I felt at ease, even though I always remained a stranger among them. Later I noticed the gap that existed between these students and the rest of the class. Still later I heard it said that I tried to pal around with the functionaries' children, which the children of the antifascists also were. However, my affinity with the antifa-kids was, first and foremost, connected with Esther. I loved her and felt secure in her company. Only much later did I become aware of a further reason for my affinity with these antifascist children, namely, the identity problems they faced in the GDR, even if these problems had different points of reference. After all, it had been Germans who had organized the mass destruction of Europe's Jews, with great conviction and German thoroughness. It had been Germans who had gassed their families. And even if the SED's leaders derived the GDR's political and moral right to exist from antifascism, postwar communists in Germany or, rather, Germans who were communists after the war, had their difficulties with the communist Jews who returned to East Germany. And the communist Jews had difficulties with their Jewishness, which they had tried to rid themselves of through assimilation. The attempt to sublimate their Jewishness into the communist movement and, further, to justify this form of assimilation using Marxist-Leninist ideology seemed to solve the Jewish question for these Jewish communists in an especially compelling way, for it encompassed a supranational sublimation of the Jewish question through international solidarity and fraternity.

Since, however, East Germany's Jewish communists were surrounded by a latent anti-Semitism even within the SED leadership, they tried especially hard to prove their socialist patriotism and affiliation. Both were constantly questioned. On the one hand, because Stalin also exploited anti-Semitism for ideological purposes. After all, it was the "uprooted cosmopolitans" with their "Zionist machinations" who periodically hampered the construction of communism through the conspiracies of worldwide Judaism. On the other hand, in the meantime, the Jewish state of Israel now existed, generously supported by the US. Consequently, during the Six Day War in 1967, communist Jews were expected to provide proofs of their loyalty by making formal statements, which they duly produced. Yet, the problem of being a Jew became a public matter again only after the East German press had published these communist Jews' statements. Why should it come as a surprise, thus, if Jewish youths, who were "children of antifascist resistance fighters" in the official political terminology, talked about how they were also Jewish children and sang ghetto songs only late in the evening when they were among themselves? And if they, like Esther, proudly wore the *keffieyeh** following the Six Day War, a feeling of self-denial still did not arise. To the contrary.

The identity problems that these children of the old communists faced on account of their past and prominent social position meant that they lived at an insurmountable distance from the "real existing" GDR.* But precisely their distance to the real situation in East Germany made my interaction with them possible. These children, whom I encountered with the other first-year students, floated over the land that their parents had presented to them as historic gift and patriotic duty for a better future. They lived detached and isolated in the country that they proudly called the German Democratic Republic. Their lives there were assured due to the "natural privileges" of their political background. Because of their parents' struggles, they too were supposed to stand at the head of the line to lead humanity to a brighter future. And even then, very few of the children of the antifascists living elsewhere in the GDR left their circle or rejected their parents' historical legacy.

The functionaries' children, whom I met in that year's class of philosophy students, accepted their parents' legacy. They were full of confidence. The future belonged to them for ever and ever. These youths were the children of history's heroes. What the parents' heroism consisted in could not be reduced to a single common denominator, though, and least of all by me. Some of them, like Esther's parents, had fought as partisans. Others had simply "just" survived emigration. If they had emigrated to the West, as a rule their survival presupposed that they had enough money to emigrate. These emigrants were mainly bourgeois, that is, middle-class intellectuals, who thanks to their worldly connections still found their way out of Nazi Germany and, thereby, escaped the gas chambers. The parents who generally had no money had emigrated to the East, and they were most likely to have been German Communist Party functionaries. They were completely at the mercy of Stalin's secret police for their survival. As is generally known, the line between the Gulag and a return to Germany was a fine one, and not just for these emigrants. Just like Esther's parents, most of the eastern émigrés who went back to the GDR contributed to the construction of Stalinist socialism* by being functionaries.

I later regarded concentration camp survivors and partisan fighters as the most authentic sorts of resistance fighters. I had doubts about the heroism of many of those who had emigrated to the West, since to me surviving outside the German hell did not unconditionally involve heroism. At the time I came into contact with the antifa-kids, however, I did not have such thoughts.

The crucial point for the children of the antifascists, that is, for the hero-children, was that the future plainly belonged to them. Consequently, they also sang the "International," and not just when they were by themselves.* For it was not just the future that belonged to them, but the future in the future, which one day would be realized as world revolution. As the children of history's putative victors, thus, they had only one single duty: to participate in the achievement of a communist future. Many of them were later destroyed by this self-same duty to become heroes.

These antifa-kids formed the core of the next generation of the elite and, thereby, the nomenklatura. They had born into their careers, not so much as a career but rather as their moral obligation to engage in the worldwide struggle for the liberation of humanity. Nikolai Ostrovsky had set forth the standard in his novel, *Wie der Stahl gehärtet wurde* (*How the Steel Was Tempered*):* "You should live so that at the end of your life you can say that you have devoted your whole life to the greatest cause of humanity: the construction of communism!" These hero-children were to sacrifice themselves for the sake of humanity. That was their historical duty, with which their parents had burdened them. In their own self-understanding, consequently, their career was not a career but a sacrifice on humanity's behalf!

Indeed, these children knew no boundaries. That too accounted for their appeal to me. For me, their detachment and unworldliness were like drugs against the real existing GDR. The longer I listened, the less I could deprive myself of it. Despite all the political knowledge and pathos, my interest in the antifa-kids was primarily something rapturous, appealing to the diffuse and romantic ideas from my previous life. For I was convinced that the world could be redeemed through music, so long as the music was sufficiently perfected and was played with utmost intensity.

Devoted though they were to the cause, the antifa-kids' interest in Marx's and Engels's writings was largely theoretical, at times even spiritual. They paid attention only to Marx's treatises on economics and his early works (*Frühschriften*). In particular, they focused on those sections of these texts that directly or indirectly dealt with the problem of alienation and its potential abolition, an alienation that, per Party resolution, did not exist under socialism. Using Marx's *Das Kapital* (*Capital*), we could discuss alienation and the secret of commodities as well as their fetish character for at least an entire academic year.

The unintended irony in spending two semesters studying commodity fetishism, of all things, in a country where there was a lack of all goods and where, consequently, an altogether different commodity fetish really existed, did not strike me at the time. We were concerned with higher things. Hence, I could soon say "we." We searched for the spiritual elements and structures of a better world, which we called "world revolution." Our attention was thus directed at a theoretical puzzle that operated under the magical phrase "Abolition of Alienation." It concerned the liberation of all of humanity, which, precisely because it was all of humanity, meant that people could not be asked individually if they even wanted to be liberated.

Yes, such global generalizations and presumptions appealed to me. For the good of all humanity perhaps it was worthwhile after all to ponder over commodity fetishism for months in our study groups. In poorly heated, dark rooms we huddled together in Humboldt University's Philosophical Institute and passionately discussed our hopes. For there was a promise for the future.

And so, I had found my crowd among my classmates and was plunging into Marx's main economic writings, which were soon joined by Hegel's *Science of Logic* and *Phenomenology of Spirit*. I was at work measuring out the theoretical space to find a place for me that I could set up according to my own terms. This niche within philosophy could be occupied without political suspicion, as long as one did one's homework in such dogmatic subjects as Socialist Theory or Socialist Ethics:

pure opportunism! At the time it was called making sacrifices for the sake of theory. And what did this entail? Loading eclectic phrases into short-term memory for an exam, so that I could recite them and forget them afterwards.

Occasionally I felt sick after completing such an ideologically highly charged exam. Then I swore at myself. At some point, though, I took a shower and washed away the socialist nonsense, or so I thought. After such exams I read with pleasure the melancholic lines from Marx's *Grundrisse* (*Outline of the Foundations of the Critique of Political Economy*) concerning the inversion of social and individual conditions. The line that became one of my favourites that year was: "This inversion is a *real phenomenon*, not a merely *supposed one*!"* In a very awkward way, I was trying to maintain contact with my true self. I was trying to send out a message that I would still be able to receive after years of being disconnected from myself, one that reminded me of how all these distortions and inversions began.

5

Apart from myself, everyone in this first group of friends that I had made in the GDR was a member of the SED. Now and again this made life within the group difficult. Much of what the others discussed in their Party meetings could not be discussed further in my presence, since, as a non-member, I was not politically mature enough to find out what Party members were allowed to know and what they discussed internally at their Party meetings. Consequently, Esther often asked me if I might also want to join the Party. She could speak to her father about it. And she did speak to him. He then talked with me. He thought that if I really exerted myself, I could succeed in ridding myself of my individualism and my petty-bourgeois tendencies. He was prepared to help me. He would sponsor my candidacy for SED membership. I was torn: on the one hand, I still had my reservations about the SED; on the other hand, I did not want to lose the group's sympathies. I spoke with Esther's father about my reservations regarding the Party. He took them in a friendly way, saying that the GDR needed just such critical people as myself. I was touched that he courted me so. For that, I liked him more than ever before. And so, it did not take a lot of prodding, from either Esther or her father, before I said yes to joining the SED.

Now and then I had doubts as to whether it was really the right thing to do, since my reservations about the Party returned at irregular intervals. When I was in the clique, the doubt disappeared. After all, we were busy constructing an objective theory for the salvation of humanity that finally would abolish alienation for everyone.

Relations between Alex and me changed with the start of my studies in Berlin. The witless and listless girlfriend had changed into a student who worked excessively and systematically. Disciplined and with a sense of purpose, I took notes on one book of philosophy after another. I had learned to work while studying piano. To practise piano for roughly four hours each day and, in addition, go to school and do whatever else was part of a musician's training: all this could only be completed with great discipline. Alex was irritated. From morning to evening I confronted him with questions: If "A" is not valid, but instead "B" is, and if "B" is not valid, but not "A" either, then how do I arrive at "C"? If, however, the colour "white" is not "white" at all, and we have only the impression that "white" is white, what then is "white"? Is a "white" even conceivable without a "black," and how would it be rendered visible? For the moment, thus, let us set aside "black" entirely, in order to concentrate on the problem …

Occasionally, Alex blew his top over my speculations. Enough with this nonsense already, he exclaimed. It really got on his nerves. If he listened to me any longer, he once said, he would end up believing that he was colour-blind. And I remember that I clapped my hands out of sheer joy and said: "That's it precisely: everything could be completely different from what we think it to be. We are the prisoners of our perceptions and habits." Alex did not always succeed in laughing then. Sometimes he stood in front of me, irritated, and mused that perhaps it was true after all that I was not quite right in the head.

Alex tried his best to understand, but speculating really was not his thing. He was an electrical engineer. He built and tinkered with accessible switches for electrical circuits at the "Plant for Signal and Safety Devices," the socialist railway yard. Alex thought concretely about solvable problems.

"World revolution" was also not his cup of tea. He was interested in cars. Since there were not any new ones in the East, he bought one used car after another and, from two vehicles, made one that worked. For days and nights on end he sat around with his friends in his mother's garden plot. And when they got one of the old clunkers to work again, they were as delighted as a bunch of little kids.

We often did not have much money at the time because some replacement part or another had to be acquired. In return, we had a Wartburg car with a Volkswagen motor.* Many people envied Alex because of that motor. But he also accepted that we lived on Knorr soups. Parsley, asparagus, and mushroom soups, Maggi bouillon cubes with vermicelli: that is what we ate the whole week long.* My grandmother soon started sending wholesale-size packages of them to us. She thought that we were selling the soup packets on the black market. In fact, we did this now and then: one soup packet for five East German marks (*Ostmark*).

In the middle of the 1960s, my grandmother finally registered herself as a West German who lived in West Berlin and could, like other West Germans, travel to the GDR. She could not do this as a West Berlin resident, because the East German authorities viewed West Berlin as an autonomous political entity, that is, a foreign country. When I saw my grandmother again, I kept secret from her that we ate the soups ourselves. She was too shocked anyway by the "hole" in which I was living. That was not quite accurate. After all, by now Alex and I had moved into a two-room apartment in a renovated older building. But my grandmother did not accept my objection. She cried hysterically after she had seen the "hole." She could never have imagined that I would be so unkempt. She remorselessly called our furniture junk and my clothes rags. Indeed, given the circumstances, she thought it was truly a miracle that I was still alive. After that first visit, she sent us abundant amounts of food packages, clothing, and household items. With all that, we could even provide for Alex's family. She sent Alex tools. He loved her for that.

Even later, I never told my grandmother that her ideas about my philosophy studies were completely off base. She did not suspect in the least that the curriculum focused on Marxist-Leninist philosophy. It simply never occurred to her. I also did not tell her that I had decided to join the SED. She would have had a breakdown, proclaiming in West Berlin and anywhere else that, on top of everything, her granddaughter had now been forced to join the Communist Party. She never would have believed that I had done it voluntarily. For the few hours that I saw her, I wanted peace with her. I loved her and she was my only link to family.

When I saw my grandmother again following the construction of the Wall, she belonged already to another world. My grandmother was part of a life that now would never be. I was stuck at the end of that life and had crawled into a hole. There was no way back. My grandmother belonged to a world that I preferred not to think about, because then tears would stream uncontrollably down my face and I would become aware of the ridiculousness of what I was doing here. For I, too, always knew that what I was doing here actually had nothing to do with me. If there was a word that best described my psychological state then, after "fearful," it was "dull." I also feared the memories of my previous life. I had not entirely managed to kill off the memories of the times before, even if I had never again touched a musical instrument seriously. For ever since I had been ejected from my musical existence, I lacked the strength, the immense amount of strength. For years I could not even listen to music. I feared that it would collapse – this makeshift world that I was building for myself after the incomprehensible end of my previous world.

I could not talk with my grandmother about this, in part because I did not understand what really had happened to me. And so I also did not tell her that, after I had been released from the psychiatric clinic, I took large doses of sleeping pills and sedatives. I did not tell her, even though she told me to my face: Child, you're sick. What did they do to you in the clinic? What are you so afraid of? I tried not to burst out crying when she posed her questions. I was glad that I began to redirect the fear into mathematical sequences, so that through concentrated effort I could suppress it for at least an hour at a time. I did not tell her that I did not pick up the strong psychotherapeutic pills that the psychiatrists were still prescribing me at all but instead procured sleep aids and weaker sedatives. For, in contrast to the strong psychotropic drugs, they did not cause me to lose touch with myself completely.

My grandmother was tactful enough to tolerate my silence, even later, after I had got used to seeing her again.

Dazed and subdued by sedatives, I burrowed in my tunnel towards a methodology for a theory of contradictions. When the pressure became too great, I called in sick. It did not take very long before I had doctors' certificates and documents proclaiming my unfitness not only for the pre-military training camp but also for harvest actions, mass parades, and other group-building exercises.

I used the time to read more intensively about the logic of contradictions and set it in relation to possible starting points for a general theory of action. While people in the Czechoslovak Socialist Republic tried to act practically in order to push for more democracy, I too was interested in "practice," but rather as a category. Defining precisely the concept of "action" seemed essential to me. Without theory, no empiricism and no revolutionary praxis – that was my arrogant and philosophically German standpoint. To dream of "socialism with a human face" seemed to me not just theoretically naïve.* In my opinion, socialism, as it existed in Czechoslovakia, the Soviet Union, or the GDR, nowhere possessed a real basis on which a human face could find a lasting foundation. A socialism that – for their own happiness – would force people behind walls with automatic firing installations* could never have a human face as far as I was concerned. Democracy and shoot-to-kill-orders for people who did not want a share in "socialist happiness" were mutually exclusive. Here was a logical flaw in the socialist theory of happiness. A theory of socialism that insists on the logical principle of "either/or," and hence rules out a third option, cannot guarantee any sort of human tolerance in its praxis. For that reason, too, I reflected on an entirely new theory, one in which multiple values and, hence, multiple standpoints and opinions could coexist on an equal footing in a single social practice. Only on the basis of such a pluralistic theoretical approach could an "entirely new socialism" finally come into existence, one that left behind the calculation of "either/or" and, with it, real existing socialism's "friend-foe principle." I believed myself to be on the way towards such a theoretical approach: an all-embracing theory, a general theory of everything that had at once Einsteinian scope and the precision of Heisenberg's uncertainty principle for boundary conditions in a theoretical field. I searched for nothing more, but also nothing less. And the reform efforts in Czechoslovakia seemed to me an experiment without any theoretical basis, as long as its proponents held on to Leninism.

Meanwhile, hopes for a socialism with a more human face rose among the antifa-kids. Not that they regarded the existing socialism as inhuman, certainly not. But it was clearly worthy of improvement: on that point they all agreed. And who should improve it, if not they? More democracy, after all, could not be detrimental to the socialist future. Naturally, the Party's leading role would have to be preserved. There was never even a minute's doubt about that. They were staunchly devoted to the Party and the state and were prepared to assume the leadership of the socialist state in the future. No wonder that they argued passionately about the Prague Spring. They rejected my theoretical pessimism towards the Prague Spring politely, yet resolutely. Within our circle of friends, Esther defended me, by promoting understanding and tolerance. She rejected my reflections, calling them "theoretical radicalism." I was blinded by theory, she said, but praxis would soon prove me wrong.

My candidacy year, during which I had to prove myself politically and demonstrate that I was mature enough to be a Party member, came to an end. Jonas really had vouched for me. I was invited with a number of other candidates to the SED's district committee office. Over coffee and cake we made small talk about this and that and about the construction of socialism, which needed students like us, we were told, for the process was difficult. It all depended on young, critical comrades.

Therefore, we shouldn't hold back with our criticisms. Without criticism, the life would go out of the Party. One by one we were asked if we saw things that needed improvement. When it was my turn, I criticized *Neue Deutschland* (New Germany), the Party newspaper. I said that stylistically it was just awful, its use of language was unbearable, and its logical reasoning, too, left much to be desired. Sometimes the tautologies came fast and thick, rendering the reports implausible and vulnerable to logical attack. They kindly let me finish speaking and asked if I had still other critical observations. No, not at the moment, I replied. They thanked us for coming and for the constructive criticism. Then we were dismissed.

The result of this nice chat was that I was not accepted into the SED. Indeed, my petty-bourgeois tendencies had been expressed all too clearly. I was told that my criticism of the "Party's Central Organ" was outrageous. Furthermore, I had demonstrated clearly with my erratic behaviour that I had not comprehended the gravity of the international political situation. I did not understand this last argument at all, since no one had asked me about the international political situation. I did understand that, for now, I would have to remain a candidate member for another year. Jonas had spoke decisively on my behalf with the faculty's Party Committee so that my candidacy was not revoked.

Conversations with Jonas followed. He said that I had to understand, had to read more about the class struggle, study Lenin, give serious attention to strategy and tactics, and work to overcome my petty-bourgeois tendencies. Otherwise he would not be able to vouch for me any longer. The study collective would help me, he promised. I really did not understand what this was all about, but I was sure that Jonas meant well by me.

Our class became politically restless. The pros and cons of reforming existing socialism were discussed more fiercely. The political dogmatists in our class stood against the reform-friendly hero-children. But the Institute's leaders did not have the nerve to proceed against the hero-children, that is, to discipline them. Instead, the university administration launched a wide variety of activities. For enthusiasm for "reformed socialism" was also growing among the students in the other departments.

This marked the beginning of a university reform. On Esther's initiative, the antifa-kids pushed for my election onto a committee to reform the lectures. My theoretical reflections could best be applied and be corrected there. I was enthusiastic. To me, reforming the lectures and the curriculum seemed the right place to start. Along with other students, I spoke up for making professors accountable for the content of their lectures. They should have to justify the purpose of the subject matter being offered and its role in the broader curriculum. They should have to explain why the particular focus they had chosen for a lecture was important for our education. Furthermore, students should have the right to choose their lectures freely and criticize the teaching method openly. For weeks, I believed that all this was really about improving the content of our education and was purely about teaching. We were working on a model for linking the lectures systematically so as to avoid repetitions and wasted time. I landed on a study commission set up by the dean of the Arts and Humanities.

Then came 21 August 1968. We were on summer break. I was working in the light bulb factory to improve my desperate financial situation. Alex had bought another used car and had racked up new debts.

At the end of the night shift, the workers became excited when the news was announced. Opinions about the Warsaw Pact countries' invasion of Czechoslovakia were divided. But even before views could be articulated, the "comrade workers" from the night shift were rounded up. They were supposed to make statements welcoming the invasion. I did not say that I was a "comrade worker who was a candidate for Party membership." Here, I was only a casual worker on the night shift. I collected my pay and then had breakfast in a pub. After eating, I did not go home. The police presence in the streets and the excitement of the workers in the light bulb factory propelled me to the university's Philosophical Institute.

It was after nine o'clock. Of my classmates, only the apparatchiks were there. By now it had dawned on me, too, that their interest in the curriculum had been motivated by political surveillance first and philosophy second. They were predominantly students who, before going to university, had voluntarily committed themselves to serve in the National People's Army for three years. This commitment arose partly out of conviction and partly out of opportunism, since the "service of honour" (*Ehrendienst*) in the People's Army, as this extended military service was officially called, promised one admission to university and a double stipend, even if the applicant's academic qualifications were substandard. They were replaced by the criterion of political reliability.

Little by little, more students and even instructors arrived. Most of them had leadership positions in either the Institute or the Party. Esther was out of town. In the course of the morning, one of Esther's friends from the group of antifa-kids arrived. We could not stand each other, not only because we could not endure each other as women, but also because we held completely opposite political views. She was a dogmatist, something that was always more difficult for me to put up with in women than in men. After 1989, Esther confessed to me that her friend had been a captain in the State Security Service (Staatssicherheitsdienst or Stasi) already in our second year. And indeed, during my studies I never could shake my suspicion that she was a Stasi informant.

I was not needed at the university. In fact, I was in the way. For the foremost concern here was the formulation of political argumentation strategies by the Party and Institute leadership, strategies aimed at having the entire student body welcome the invasion. Esther's friend told me that I could go home, although I should stay available in the case of an emergency. She would call me if I were needed.

Of course, I was not indifferent to the invasion of "friendly troops" who, in a spirit of friendship, shot their friends. Of course, I was outraged that tanks and armies had brought the Prague Spring to a violent end. But, in contrast to others, I had not expected anything! After all, in the construction of the Berlin Wall I had already experienced a demonstration of military violence from which I had never recovered. I had no hope at all that a more human face could ever endure under real existing socialism, whether in East Germany or elsewhere. I had been working for a long time on the theoretical justification of my insight that nothing could be changed anyway. I was working at expressing my fatalism in philosophical propositions. I began to theorize the violence done to me when the Wall went up as well as my helplessness in the face of these events in terms of immutable laws that existed independently of my wants and desires. To me, the events in Czechoslovakia only confirmed my fatalistic approach. Recognizing the objective laws of history was the most one could do; nothing could alter its course. Therefore, any attempt to intervene was pointless and, at most, satisfied character types with a pathological need to help, with their childish fantasies of omnipotence acted out in class struggle games. It was just not possible to go against the unalterable course of history. With this "philosophical depression," as I later called it, I soon had all the mental qualifications to be a good philosopher of history, who could invoke Marx as well as Hegel. Reason in history! It is inevitable and will thus find its way logically and consistently. It will pass over real existing socialism just as it does real, existing capitalism. It will unfold in the world historical process with inexorable necessity.

I had thus found a faith and was on the way to paving it with every manner of philosophical argument. Sentence by sentence, I wanted to bring it to light from the well of the objective logic of being.* In this context, the Prague Spring was only a puzzle that confirmed that it is not possible to intervene actively in history. Once again, I had succeeded in fleeing from the real world.

Meanwhile, and to my astonishment, people at the university were talking about my sense of political responsibility. In a politically decisive situation I had known where I was supposed to be. By showing up at the university on the day when the counterrevolution had been checked through the Warsaw Pact countries' decisive intervention, I had acted in a politically conscious manner. I did not contradict them. I did not say that I had come from the night shift at the light bulb factory and only out of pure curiosity had walked to the Philosophical Institute. I also did not say that I was wholly indifferent to the socialist reforms.

Instead, I debated the deployment of tanks in Prague all the more intensely with Esther. I all but blamed her personally for the entry of the troops, who shot defenceless people in their "glorious struggle." Esther was caught in a contradiction: on the one hand, Party discipline required her to defend the invasion as a matter of principle; on the other, however, she spoke out in favour of the socialist reforms. She criticized precisely how the Party leaders had choked off all discussion of the invasion and the Prague reform efforts. We debated for nights on end without ever agreeing on anything.

As a result, communication between Esther and me became more difficult in the weeks that followed. She did not tell me that, with some others from our circle, she was involved in writing a letter that called for discussing openly the questions of the reforms in the Czechoslovakian People's Republic and the necessity of the socialist fraternal army's invasion of Prague. I was frustrated that I learned about the protest letter only at the student assembly. I accused Esther of not trusting me. She corrected me: trusted yes, just not in political matters. In that sense, she was right, because I did behave unpolitically. There it was: the dividing line between us and the boundary between me and the antifa-kids. In such political situations, the distance between them and myself, which I otherwise liked, suddenly turned into a foreignness that excluded me from the group. I reacted aggressively against the two judgments and the two truths: one for the politically enlightened, and one for the yet-to-be enlightened remainder, who still had to be educated.

As long as I lived in the GDR, and even after I had already given up my academic career, I belonged to those who still had not understood. That this practice of having two truth values was the foundation of political domination, I comprehended late.

Within the class, a scandal broke out once the protest letter had been made known. For the hero-children were not the only ones protesting. Other, less privileged students also had problems with the invasion. There were demands for people to make statements and declare their belief in the Party's policies and the socialist alliance with the Warsaw Pact states. Because of my appearance at the university on 21 August, I was classified with the students who had realized the seriousness of the political situation. I did not comment on this finding. My silence contributed considerably to my not being expelled during the weeks that followed. Some of the unprivileged students, though, were expelled. I called in sick and pored over Hegel's works and Marx's *Grundrisse*.

Owing to her father's political position, the Institute administration did not dare expel Esther. She was transferred "for disciplinary reasons" to the university's Institute for Marxism-Leninism. Two, three months later, the university confirmed her as a research student. This meant that she could begin doctoral work already in her third year of studies and graduate three years later without having to take the state exam. Of course, only the university's best students were allowed to do this. "Research studies" was one of the many absurd innovations of the higher education reform movement; it was scrapped a few years later. It represented a chance for Esther to survive at the university. Only with considerable difficulty, however, were the less privileged students allowed to continue their studies, if at all.

Now I was alone in my class. A harsher political wind blew through the Institute. My favourite professor, Wolfgang Heise, who taught the history of philosophy and aesthetics, was also caught up the wave of political cleansing. He was supposed to state his political position on the events in Prague. Since he also reacted to politically compromising situations with illness, his case was tried at a time when I was "healthy" again. I did not stand a chance of dodging the meeting. He was accused of every sort of political deviance. I raised my hand and wanted to defend him, which I did very poorly. I broke out in tears and bawled until the break came. During the break, he came to me and said warmly, but with great sternness, that if I didn't stop crying immediately and didn't come forward and speak up, he would never say another word to me. I obeyed – and "obeyed" was indeed the right word. I obeyed the father figure that he always was for me. He fled the Philosophical Institute. That is, he moved to the Institute for Aesthetics, voluntarily, as people stressed. From there he continued to protect me and put me on the right path philosophically. He taught me what a philosophical question is, taught me how to differentiate actual from apparent problems, and how to do honest scholarly work. All my papers, including my doctoral thesis and my first book on Hegel, passed through his hands.

Eventually I was invited once more to have a conversation with the Party, since my additional year as a candidate had run out. Again, there was coffee and cake. Again, they asked us candidates if we had suggestions for improving the way towards "developed socialism."* When it was my turn, they asked me about Christa Wolf. They had heard that I eagerly discussed her book, *Nachdenken über Christa T.* (*The Quest for Christa T.*). Politically, this was a catch-22, although, at the time, I had not even thought about that. If you said that Christa Wolf's book was good, you were considered politically unsophisticated. I did not just find the book good, I found it very good and blurted out my opinion. The book was exceptional for East Germany not only for its language but also for its content: a woman who tries to get down to business with herself and who wants to assert her rights – if need be failing in her attempt – and this under socialism. Christa T.'s death was not pointless, I asserted. She did not want to give up on herself. Even in socialism, I continued, the individual should have a right to self-determination, even if it costs one one's life. This is, after all, what we find portrayed in classic German literature, whose heritage we invoke.

The result of my emotional declaration for an individual's right to self-determination to the point of one's own death was that, once again, I was not admitted into the Party. In socialism, after all, there was no reason to die senselessly, so ran their all-encompassing argument. I did not say anything more, not even that I had tried twice already to die under this very socialism. This was all pointless, wasted energy, that much I understood. Since that conversation, I no longer had any desire to join the Party, which I also told them.

To my amazement, I was not dropped as a candidate. Once again, Jonas had spoken with the Institute administration. He did not even get angry at me, which astonished me. He just said that one could not say such things in that way. I had to learn to say what I wanted to say in a way that did not leave me open to attack. In the end, he pointed out, one could say anything – apart from inflammatory remarks against the state. I just finally had to learn how. After that, he spoke with me a lot about strategy and tactics and gave me Lenin's *What Is to Be Done* and *Left-Wing Communism: An Infantile Disorder* to read.

I discussed with my favourite professor whether I should withdraw my application to join the SED. He was strictly against it. He said that a scholar could decide not to join the SED, but it was impossible to withdraw one's application for membership. That would end any chance I had of being a scholar. Now I had to see things through, whether I wanted to or not. Unless I wanted to give up on my goal of "scholarship," which he personally believed would be a shame, since I had something like a sixth sense for theory. Consequently, I should pull myself together; after all, philosophy needed theorists just now.

So I pulled myself together. I studied silently for the state exam. Before I was allowed to graduate, I was summoned again to the SED district committee office. Now I was ready. I had understood. During this next round of the membership process, I abstained from making any sort of criticism in front of my comrades. I had acquired a cynical attitude towards my Party membership. My entry into the Party, thus, actually marked my exit. After having set the university record by being a candidate for three years – one year was usual – I had passed the test. I was finally mature enough to join the "church." At the same time, I was disgusted by my compromises, the "sacrifices" for scholarship, as I had rationalized them.

I wrote my senior thesis on "The Concept of Work in Hegel" in seclusion. To graduate, I also had to agree, in writing, that I would go wherever the Party sent me. Of course, I knew that I would not go anywhere I did not also want to go. So, during my senior year I looked for a job that involved research. My favourite professor gave me the tip that I should inquire at the Academy of Sciences (Akademie der Wissenschaften). At the time, its Institute for Philosophy was led by two directors of equal standing. I called on the director who I had heard had been a pastor before coming over to Marxist-Leninist philosophy. I had the idea that I probably had the best chance of being understood by a former pastor who, while a prisoner of war in Russia, had converted to communism through the efforts of the National Committee for a Free Germany (Nationalkomitee Freies Deutschland). And that is indeed what happened. From Gregorian chant and the development of the solo voice to Hegel, we identified a number of questions on which I would want to work. With a provisional contract for the Academy and the fatherly advice to include Lenin in my research program, I left him.

At the Philosophical Institute, meanwhile, a more dogmatic course had set in. There were personnel changes. To strengthen the Institute politically, the Ministry of University Affairs had appointed a director for education and development. He did not even have a doctorate, but was a tough Stasi agent. I could not get around him. He had to sign the preliminary contract that I had received from the Academy's Institute for Philosophy. For without his signature, there was no chance of me starting at the Academy of Sciences. The Directorate for Education and Development, however, had come up with the plan of sending me to a technical school in Cottbus. For my own benefit, I was to teach Marxism-Leninism there and thereby also become better acquainted with philosophy's fundamental practical questions. If I performed my work respectably there for two years, I was informed, the question of whether I might pursue a doctorate on a theoretical problem could be considered. First, though, I absolutely had to have more practical experience. I remained silent. But I knew that I would not go to Cottbus just to gain practical experience. I would rather work in the light bulb factory again.

I hit upon the idea that saved me when I heard that the director for education and development occasionally drank too much. I came up with the plan to obtain his signature during an end-of-semester party. I drank and flirted with him the entire evening; at least, flirted as well as one could with a man who was anything but likeable. Thanks to my time as a barmaid, I knew how to act as if I were drinking along. Then later, I took my preliminary contract, which I had carefully folded, out of my pocket and very casually asked if he wouldn't mind putting his signature to it on the lower left. And that is what he did, without paying attention to what he was signing. I stuck the piece of paper back in my pocket and refilled our wine glasses.

I took the contract to the Academy first thing the next day. Weeks later, when the director for education and development summoned me to his office, we had a heated argument about how the contract had been signed. I said that the director was so drunk that he no longer knew what he was signing. If he wanted that to become public knowledge, I offered, he could contest it. But one would then have to discuss how the comrade director was unable to maintain his political vigilance under the influence of alcohol. Alternatively, he could forget the whole thing and let me go. I promised that I would keep my mouth shut. The contract, however, lay secure at the Academy of Sciences. He was beside himself with rage. I would regret this, he roared. He threw me out of his office and never returned to the matter again.

The more I came to terms with philosophy, the more I became estranged from Alex. For a while, though, it looked to me as if we were becoming closer. During our first years together, Alex had resisted responding to my philosophical questions, but now he discussed them with me. Only sometimes did he still beg me to stop posing my metaphysical questions. He just could not bear them, he complained. Then for a while I also remained quiet, but at some point they burst out of me again.

One evening – it was just before my senior thesis defence – I enthusiastically read out loud to Alex something from Hegel's early writings: "But perhaps life cannot be regarded as union or relation alone, but must be regarded as opposition as well ... Love can take place only against its equal, against a mirror, against the echo of our own being."* Alex jumped up, turned off the soccer match he had been watching on television, and threw a fit. I'm fed up with all this philosophy crap, he raged. After a while he cried and said that his thoughts were all tangled up. He really did not know anymore if his name was Alex, or if he was just hallucinating that that was his name. He also did not know anymore if "up" was really "up" and not "down." He felt as if he would go mad at any moment. He wasn't interested anymore in what happened, if anything at all were to happen. Alex shook fiercely, then collapsed in tears. I could not even bring myself to say that it was actually wonderful that he had finally understood that our knowledge and, hence, our certainties were open to question, and that, consequently, we can state with some certainty what is valid only within a predefined space. And that he thus finally understood what was at stake when it came to being and essence.

I did not say it anymore. For a moment I understood that Alex was too healthy mentally for my metaphysical games of despair, with which I tried to ignore the real world because the world in which I lived was still unbearable to me. I understood that if I could do anything for Alex, then it would be to leave him alone and see that he found his way back to his healthy and concrete world. And ultimately, that meant separation.

I tried to calm Alex that evening, but was unsuccessful. I called his sister. With the help of sedatives we got him through the night. Since he was still crying the next morning, we called a doctor. Alex was admitted to a psychiatric clinic. He stayed there eight weeks.

I felt tremendously guilty for not having noticed how seriously I had messed Alex up. I visited him as often as I could. The doctors said that

I should cut back on my visits, since Alex reacted to them with agitation and depressive resentment. His sister discussed the possibility of a separation. We arrived at a friendly divorce. I did not feel good.

With a university degree in my pocket, thirty still a long way off, and twice divorced already, I began my work at the end of 1970 as a research assistant at the Philosophical Institute of the German Academy of Sciences.

6

In my search for a place where I could be politically out of reach, I earned a degree in philosophy. In my search for an explanation of the world, I had passed all the socialists' tests of "opportunist consensus." I had learned to divide my life into a true and a false part. In the false life, I did whatever was necessary for the sake of the cause. And the cause was still this: the search for a sensible theory.

Finding meaning so that I did not lose my mind. In the realm of theory, not only did what I think about come out true if I tossed it around in my head long enough. In this fictitious realm, the helplessness that had left me speechless also evaporated. The laws of a logical world applied here, which daily politics could not shake. In this period when I believed in theoretical infallibility, of course, I had no idea that I was practising a faith. Only years later did I realize that I had searched the volumes of Hegel's *Logic* for the genesis of the "absolute spirit," which Hegel also called "God" – and not by accident. Just as the faithful of other confessions looked in the Torah or in the Gospels, I wanted to be certain of God's existence. I searched for an echo to which I could return, whatever happened.

In short, I was looking for God in the form of an absolute, a pure theory. It would be big enough to be able to withstand the contradictions of the present and those of the past. Because, for too long now I had not known what my purpose in life was, in part because there was no end in sight. There was no stopping, just overlapping separations and now, again, separation from Alex.

To pave the path with reason! To reduce the body's complaints to zero. To look away for so long that I no longer saw myself in my face.

This is how I now wanted to handle myself: to cover the bright day with categories and concepts, in part because I did not know what heaven was good for, if there was apparently no place for me in it.

I had been received, thus, into the holy family of philosophers. In the venerable halls of the Academy of Sciences, which Leibniz had founded and the Humboldt brothers made prestigious and honourable,* I began to expand my hideout.

At the time, I was not interested in the political function of an Institute for Philosophy at the Academy of Sciences, which, as it happened, was one of the least politicized of all the state institutes for philosophy. That the Academy of Sciences was the country's largest research institution, with over twenty-five thousand employees working at more than fifty central institutes, occurred to me only after 1989. Even I knew, though, that commissions from the state were the basis for the research there. And while I had heard that the SED Central Committee itself drew up the research projects for the social science institutes, it just did not interest me.

I did not want to know that the Institute for Philosophy was one of the important sites for legitimating SED politics. I would have to come to terms with this knowledge. To me, the Institute was the most civilized institution for philosophy in East Germany, which, academically speaking, was also true. It was the civilian window-dressing, which in East Germany was precisely philosophy's function within the social sciences. Here is where the politics of the SED were made socially acceptable to Western countries.

But I did not think about such things then. My wish was to disappear into the Division for the History of Philosophy, so that I would not have to involve myself in the much less serious daily political-philosophical business.

Rather, I thought about how I would get along with my colleagues at the Institute. Since college graduates had been permitted to conduct their doctoral research at the Academy only two years before, in 1971 I was one of the first of these students. The average age of my colleagues was in the fifties. My role as the "little one" ensued almost naturally, although I was already twenty-six. I was inundated with motherly and fatherly advice: I should eat more and sleep more and not read too late at night, since, when I walked the venerable halls, I was always pale. This role was extremely comfortable. My unrehearsed, academic behaviour made it all the easier for me to play the game.

As best I could, I tried to escape my colleagues' attention. That was easily arranged. For this research institution was unusual in that, owing to a lack of space, the research staff largely had to work at home. There were only the so-called "presence days," which every staff member had to observe. This meant that everyone had to show up at the Academy twice each week. Needless to say, this was great; no one was interested in what I did. At the beginning, I felt as if I was permanently on vacation, and was even paid for it.

Two weeks after my appointment, I found papers in my box to sign concerning the "pension plan for scholars" and broke into a fit of laughter. The juxtaposition of the words "intelligence" and "pension" in the secretary's cover note was too comical. I had never imagined that one could receive a pension for one's intelligence. The personnel officer, a staunch Stasi-woman with hair dyed ash-blond, bristled at my giggling. I know now that my laughing should have driven from my head the notion that the Academy could be my final destination. But my colleagues explained that it was quite a privilege to have this type of pension, since it was more generous than the normal one.

When I left the Academy after ten years of pure academic existence there, the personnel office cold-heartedly reclaimed the privilege I enjoyed as a "philosopher in the civil service," namely my green insurance card for the "intelligence benefit."

My first work assignment at the Institute for Philosophy was intended as a punishment. I was to draw up a subject index for the forty volumes of Lenin's *Works*, which had to include the terms "working class," "class struggle," "class consciousness," and "the masses." The former pastor, at this time still one of the Institute's two autonomous directors, said that he had given me this assignment because I needed to reflect more precisely on what these terms meant. He had heard from the university that I would need to be worked with politically. This was also convenient for him, since he would soon be writing an "Outline of the History of Marxist-Leninist Philosophy." He thought that by recording the instances of these words in the forty volumes, I could learn something for my life. And the year that he allotted me for the project would help bring me along. I could come to him with my questions, whenever I wished. Then after this year, he said, we could speak about a project on Hegel. Using Lenin's *Philosophical Notebooks*, I would also be able to familiarize myself with those of Hegel's ideas that were most important for Marxism-Leninism. This was the revenge for the signature of the director for education and development at Humboldt University on my work contract.

I practised speed reading and recording individual words without taking in their content. At night I went to work in the light bulb factory again. I was working off my portion of the debts that Alex had incurred from his used cars. I thought that if I helped to pay off the debts, I could also clear away some of the guilt I felt towards him. My relations with the other women who worked on the assembly line were good. Our collegiality expressed itself by agreeing not to work faster than was necessary, by organizing smoking breaks, and – whenever a conveyor belt broke down again or there weren't any bulbs to pack – by playing skat* or poker for a tenth of a cent per point to pass the time. We also all agreed that we could take for ourselves as many of the people's light bulbs as we needed, thereby putting into practice the principle "from each according to their ability, to each according to their need."

One day I arrived for my so-called "presence day" at the Academy bleary-eyed from the night shift. A colloquium on the topic of "alienated work" had been scheduled. The breakfast that I had eaten in the factory canteen – scrambled eggs with bacon – lay heavy in my stomach. And my colleague was explaining, with considerable philosophical effort, that objectively there could not be any alienation under socialism. I played with the idea of saying that I had just come from the night shift and still heard the sound of alienated work. But I restrained myself and, well-behaved, proposed that within the context of a solidarity action we should arrange to work either a night or a day shift at the Narva light bulb factory and then donate our earnings. By working at the factory itself, we could see whether the activity was alienating or not. Some of my colleagues were unsure if I was making fools of them, for no one here knew that I spent my nights at Narva. The colleague giving the lecture on the topic was the first to regain his composure and told me that I could not combine theory and practice so mechanically. I did not say anything more and tuned out. In my head, the differences between the night and the day shifts were dissolving into dance steps that lacked a libretto. My notebook from that period was full of such dance steps and figures for a ballet in which I wanted to bring together what stood separately by itself: assembly-line work and "pure reason."*

After a little more than a year, I had worked off my portion of the debt for the used cars that Alex had bought. Money was now coming regularly into my chequing account, so I could discontinue my night shifts at the light bulb factory.

Since I could not get the dance steps and the idea of a libretto out of my head, I often attended the ballet rehearsals at the Komische Oper* in the mornings of my "presence days." I soon realized that the presence days at the Academy were a formality. It sufficed to put your briefcase down on time in the morning, spread out some reference books on the table, and say that you were going to the library and would be back by lunch at the latest. Since, with six philosophers of history sharing an office, no one could consider working at the Academy anyway, it was enough if one person stayed there who could say, if asked, that the others were away tending to this or that matter. This was necessary because, at irregular intervals, the Institute administration conducted attendance checks. This was a bit reminiscent of school, and so the co-workers behaved accordingly. One person covered for everyone else. In this way it was possible, within certain limits, for the individual staff members to organize their presence days at the Institute for Philosophy as they saw fit. Some went shopping, others in fact went to the library or to a café. I went to Café Espresso, where half the Institute congregated on the presence days, or I went to the rehearsals at the Komische Oper. It was right in the neighbourhood. There I learned about the Young Dancers group (Junge Tänzer), and applied to join. For years during my other, musical life, I had also had ballet lessons. That would be enough for the group dance if I practised regularly. At some point, I naïvely asked to be excused from a Party meeting because the ballet rehearsal was about to begin – and was not allowed to leave. The Party secretary then confronted me, in all seriousness, with the choice: either dance or become a philosopher. The two were not compatible with one another. I tried to explain that Marx himself had spoken about how, among other things, free existence consisted in being able to go fishing in the morning, till the fields at midday, and pursue philosophical criticism in the evening.* Since my comments were interpreted as politically immature, I sought out a politically more mature excuse for the next time.

During this period, I came up with the idea of transforming Hegel's *Phenomenology of Spirit* into a ballet. I searched the text for potential dance steps and found them too. I preferred to work on my libretto during the Institute's endless meetings. Since we had a lot of meetings, the ballet was taking shape nicely until one afternoon. I was abruptly pulled from my daydream and the yawning boredom changed suddenly and unexpectedly into a drama. Three Furies, dressed as politicians, were pulling to pieces the man who, along with my pastor, served as the Institute's co-director. Even I knew that this other co-director was the real head of the Institute, but at the time I did not want to know anything more, partly because I got on well with my former pastor. As I later learned, these crazed women had been charged by the SED district leadership to bring down the real head of the Institute. Their performance was staged. Before long, a hysterical lynching mood developed that was so disgusting that there was hardly any air left to breathe. The meeting lasted more than seven hours. When it was through, I walked the streets for hours and howled about all the malicious behaviour. At some point, I began picking a giant bouquet of fall flowers from the city's flowerbeds. That calmed me. The bouquet was very beautiful. I looked up the Institute director's address in a phone booth, walked to Alexanderplatz, and rang his doorbell. He opened the door himself. Without saying a word, I handed him the bouquet. Without saying a word, he invited me into the kitchen and made me a cup of cocoa, on which I warmed my hands. Only then did I notice that I was freezing. He laid a blanket over me and sat down. Everything transpired without us ever saying a word. We sat at the kitchen table until it got light out outside. Then he called a taxi and said that it would probably be better now if I slept for a few hours.

From that evening, a deep sense of understanding joined us in a silence that we absolutely wanted to preserve. It had something to do with an admission of helplessness. There was a language underneath language that we had found together. We both knew that this silence was unique and for that reason we never got any closer to one another. This silence protected me at the Academy in the coming years. For, having surviving the power play, he later became the sole, commanding director, indeed one of the most feared directors of all time at the Academy of Sciences. He was one of the most intelligent and sophisticated intriguers that I ever met in East Germany. But he always kept me out of everything. Whereas he soon demanded that all other staff members submit unconditionally to his policies for the Institute, he only demanded from me this distance in which the silence of that night at the kitchen table recovered its sound.

The "Lenin Year" drew to a close. I had my hands full, since I had severely underestimated the amount of time needed to prepare the index. I asked two of the Institute's research assistants to help me generate the index and paid them for their work. They filled out index cards for me while on the job at the Institute. I made the deadline just by the skin of my teeth. The index was in three different hands, but the former pastor never once spoke to me about it. When he retired three years later, I fetched the five boxes of index cards from his office. They had been put aside with other papers to be picked up with the recycling. Later, I gathered the metaphors and citations for my novel *Nächte mit Hegel* (Nights with Hegel) on the backs of these index cards.

I had to change my work habits: this was the only thing that completing the index had taught me.

I had managed to come terms with things at Institute for Philosophy a little and had met my co-workers. Among them was Carla. She was fifteen years older and was incessantly theorizing on the dialectical law of "the negation of the negation," with which she wanted to overturn everything. Like me, she had the idea that we could change the world with theory, as long as the theory was constructed well enough.

Carla was from the countryside and, in her attitude, remained very much a country girl. Her eyes shone when she picked berries to make jam. She was happy when we found mushrooms in the forest that she could prepare for supper. I often asked Carla how she ended up in philosophy, of all things. She did not understand my question. In such moments she looked at me as if I were a creature from another planet and, in the end, dismissed the question with friendly, maternal laughter. To her, I was a talented theorist – even if my head was in the clouds – and she wanted to protect me, which she did.

I frequently did not know where I should go outside of my academic life. The philosophy that I had got into did not solve even one of my questions about the why and wherefore. To the contrary, it pulled me ever deeper into something that I actually did not believe. Over the years I had indeed learned to give an answer to nearly every question. The appalling thing about this, though, was that the answers did not help me get through the night. Years passed before I understood that, from its very foundation, this philosophy was useless for life; indeed, by definition it was not made for a single individual. To the contrary. There was no place for the individual within so-called Marxist-Leninist philosophy. Indeed, it held that the concrete, individual person was to be sacrificed for the greater good, a million times over if necessary, just as Stalin had done.

7

I had not just learned to divide my life into a false and a true part. I had learned to divide it into multiple false and multiple true parts. And I have lived these divisions. The more I understood how to work with definitions and their applicability, the more successful I was in separating my life from my life. I stopped talking about alienation. I was soon living it with increasing virtuosity.

Only at night, just before I fell asleep, did the many existences start to recombine. Every now and again, I sprang from the bed and took a sleeping pill, sometimes two. When they did not help, I went with my fear to some bar or another. In just such a late-night bar I met Emanuel. We talked until the place closed. Emanuel took me home and stayed. He made breakfast for me the next morning and stayed. He turned on the heating, went shopping, and stayed. It was love out of exhaustion. He cooked dinner for me. It was the first warm meal I had had in weeks. It was love and exhaustion. I called him Emanuel from the beginning, even though his name was Thomas. He did not object to me calling him by his middle name. Emanuel stayed for I don't know how many days. We hadn't counted them. Then he said that he had to go to take care of some things and that he would be back in about four weeks. One month later he stood in the doorway with his desk and countless boxes of books.

We loved each other and worked a lot. Emanuel had until spring to complete his dissertation. During that period, I began to write down this and that purely for my own understanding. Then I put these things up for discussion in our work group. It greatly impressed my colleagues that "the little one" had written thirty pages in so little time. The content of what I had written was relatively uninteresting.

Important, though, was the number of pages – that was a fetish at the Institute, as I soon comprehended. I gave up my thing about having to save paper. I set my typewriter to double-spacing and divided up my pages more generously. I gained a reputation for working a lot. Similar quantitative criteria also applied at the library. There people counted how many books each staff member borrowed. So I frequently dragged home suitcases full of books and then returned them to the Institute and earned the reputation: The little one is industrious and reads a lot. As a result, people pretty much left me alone.

The coming winter brought Emanuel and me even closer together. We did not need much; above all, no explanations of any sort. We were enough for each other. We also had enough coal to get through the winter. When spring arrived, Emanuel suggested that we get married. It was a good idea. We got married, told no one about it, and travelled to Prague.

After we had returned, I resolved to see to my dissertation more seriously. I was determined to resign from the Institute if I could not work on Hegel. I had already spoken with my favourite professor. He wanted me to work on linear and nonlinear temporal structures in music. He had wanted that for years. He was also trying to obtain a position for me. Determined, now that my punishment project on Lenin was finished, to return to real philosophy even at the Institute for Philosophy, I went to the Institute soon after returning from our honeymoon. I notified the personnel department of my new last name. The name was difficult to write, but I would master it soon enough.

I was asked if I was somehow connected to Jürgen Kuczynski. Confident, I said no. His name was Emanuel, actually Thomas even. In fact, I did not even know who Jürgen Kuczynski was, since I did not read a daily paper, nor even the weeklies. For years, I had not been able to shed my aversion to political jargon. Thankfully, I did not need any newspaper for my specialty: Hegel and pure theory. And since Jürgen Kuczynski had never published anything on Hegel, I did not even recognize his name from the secondary literature.

The questions about Jürgen Kuczynski kept coming up. I could sincerely answer that I did not know him. At some point Emanuel had told me something about his parents. But it was entirely incidental, indeed so incidental, just as when I talked about my parents, that I had concluded that Emanuel made as little of his parents as I did of mine. That was just right for me.

Hardly eight days after I had notified the Institute of my new last name, the Institute director, who now ran things without a co-director, called me to his office. It was the first time we had spoken to one another since our evening meeting at his kitchen table. On his chair lay my thesis and a final essay from my third year of classes. He told me that they had both been well written. And the thesis in particular betrayed an astonishing capacity for abstraction as well as linguistic talent. The voice that spoke to me here was one of the numerous fatherly voices that I knew from my still rather unkempt life. Why hadn't I stayed with Hegel, he asked? Before I found an answer, he suggested that I expand my thesis into a dissertation. He would advise it. In four months I was to make an appointment to see him again and present some ideas for the topic. Afterwards silence hung again in the room. For a moment we listened to it. Then he stood up, took his leave from me without saying a word, and brought me to the door. I had just about left the office when he called to me that I should say hello to Jürgen Kuczynski for him.

As soon as I was standing in the hall of the Institute again, I started to feel dizzy. Then I felt compelled to visit the Academy's library. I looked up the name Kuczynski in the alphabetical catalogue and was surprised by the number of titles: they went on and on. When I arrived home I asked Emanuel if his father's name was Jürgen. Downplaying it, he said yes and that we were invited to dinner on Friday. When I asked why he had never told me that his father had written such a large number of books, he said dryly that I had never asked about it.

Later I learned that Emanuel's first marriage had gone to pieces because his wife was more interested in the famous name than she was in Emanuel. Hence, it had suited Emanuel well that I did not know anything about his privileged family.

The Friday evening came when we were invited to dinner. I was a bit irritated when I realized: a family gathered here that always gathered here on Fridays. The family was rather large and I was the newcomer. Now I understood why Emanuel often did not have time for us on Friday night.

"Nice of you to come," Emanuel's father greeted me. "Thomas has already told us a lot about you, my dear. How was the trip to Prague? Were you in the castle? Did you see Rodin's statue of St John the Baptist in the National Gallery's garden?" "Isn't it lovely?" his mother asked.

Emanuel was very pleased and talked away. As the newcomer, I was led into the dining room. I was not prepared for the whole family thing.

There was much here that reminded me of my grandmother: the Meissen porcelain, the silverware, the weave of the cloth napkins, the larded fillet of beef. I had forgotten that there were even such things as larding needles. The silverware rests on the damask tablecloth – they really seemed unreal and came across to me as staged. In addition, there was the chandelier from the eighteenth or nineteenth century above the table and chairs. All this in the middle of East Berlin. A venerable house full of furniture from various centuries and books from three generations, as I soon learned. When I entered the house I had already noticed the collection of Liebermanns in the hall.* I later learned that they were all originals.

The conversation at the table was the continuation of countless prior conversations. The topics ran from Aristotle through Turgot* to current politics and the latest resolutions of the umpteenth SED Party Conference, at which Erich Honecker's* speech was considered especially good. The conversation then turned to the Academy of Sciences, since the Council for Social Sciences had just met. The Central Committee of the SED found that …

I did not exactly comprehend what I had stumbled into, but I did understand that I had stumbled into a place where I had no business being. There was this peculiar disparity between the finest chocolate mousse, which, in an earlier time, I had eaten at my grandmother's, and the praise for Honecker's last speech, which had been so brilliant. On the wall of the dining room hung an original Käthe Kollwitz.* I could not put the puzzle together. A feeling of trepidation arose within me as well as irrepressible anger, in which there was also hatred. Here was, in short, the bourgeois version of the East German elite. They could bring together chocolate mousse, Liebermann, and the stupidity of an Erich Honecker in a conversation without ever choking on their fillet of beef. When my mother-in-law, whom I had just met, asked whether I wanted another glass of Chianti, I threw my red wine glass across the table and screamed something about red aristocracy, brilliant, and this in the middle of East Berlin. Then I burst out crying. Very calmly my new mother-in-law said that if I didn't feel well I could go upstairs and lie down in her room. She asked Emanuel to show me the way. I threw another fit. I did not need to lie down. Seeing all this here just made me want to throw up. Furious, I left the house.

Very despondently, Emanuel followed after me. I did not try to make any excuses and thought that my outburst had taken care of the issue of "family."

The next day my mother-in-law called and asked whether I was doing better. She had been worried and had not slept well. She said that if I did not want to, naturally, I did not have to come to the family dinners. She and Jürgen would understand. She was worried about my physical condition, though. My nerves didn't seem to be the strongest. Moreover, Emanuel had told her that I also didn't sleep very well. She said that whenever I wished she would be happy to discuss it with me; perhaps together we could find a way. But, of course, only when it was okay with me. So, take care, my dear. We'll wait for your call. Our greetings to Emanuel.

I was irritated. With my spontaneous performance, I had hoped to be rid of the "family" issue. Emanuel's parents had chosen voluntarily to come to East Germany after being émigrés in England. They had decided for themselves to make their intellectual abilities available for constructing a socialist East Germany. They were doubly privileged, for they were bourgeois intellectuals in the third or fourth generation and, for that reason, infinitely superior to all the intellectuals at the workers' and peasants' universities who had been stamped out quickly. Furthermore, after emigrating from England, they had arrived as Jewish antifascists in East Germany, where antifascism had been decreed a legitimating ideology for the construction of socialism.

I had married into one of the most privileged families of East Germany. Hardly anyone believed me when I said I knew nothing about the Kuczynski family. Carla, yes. She also advised me not to justify myself any longer. It would not improve the situation. I would have to endure it and learn to differentiate between flattery and sincere interest in me. There were very contrary reactions to my marriage, however, at the Academy. One set was made up of those who tried to get chummy with me, kissing my hand and sending greetings to my father-in-law with best regards. Then there were those who cut themselves off from me personally and never greeted me again. For them, I had simply risen into the ruling orthodoxy with which they wanted nothing to do. After all, Jürgen Kuczynski was already at the time frequently writing the economic portions of Honecker's speeches. I felt sympathetic towards the co-workers who avoided me. Still, my sympathy did not help me get over my isolation from those co-workers who were interested in constructing philosophical theories. They no longer trusted me anymore.

I was no longer myself. I was the daughter-in-law and did not know how to handle that. What I wrote, I now wrote as the daughter-in-law.

What I said acquired political importance. Whether I wanted it or not, I belonged to a social institution named Kuczynski. Friendly relationships frequently proved to be just a tactical connection. At some point the question eventually arose: Couldn't you just try to ... ? I was a member of a political clan. People credited me with having power. But in fact I could not do anything except for myself. Whenever I brought anyone else's concern to my father-in-law, I always heard the same phrase from him: that person should come to me directly instead of bothering you.

I never really came to terms with the fact that I suddenly belonged to the most privileged stratum of East German society. Deep within me was my hatred towards everything that this country represented. But then there was my love for Emanuel. His family had begun to worry sincerely about me. My mother-in-law looked after my health with great dedication. Soon she had organized an entire team of doctors who occupied themselves with restoring my body, which had been weakened by exhaustion. I was referred to the Baumann Clinic, whose doors were closed to the average East German citizen. The doctors here were charged with my rehabilitation. During my stays in the clinic I not only encountered my Institute director in the mornings, but also my doctoral advisor in his blue bathrobe. Without saying a word we went our way to the same laboratory and knew that the privilege of being treated here joined us in a special way. I encountered there famous artists, architects, sculptors, and scholars; in short, the privileged stratum of the country as well as those segments of the nomenklatura who were not treated at the government hospital or the Stasi's special clinics (which were built later on).

Since I did not want to have anything to do with the circle of the powerful, I was thrown back hopelessly on myself. Even friends like Carla were more guarded towards me than before. No matter how much she stuck by me, she still carefully chose the information she gave me.

Two or three years ago, when I saw her again, Carla told me that she had read Koestler's *Darkness at Noon* in 1973* and that, since then, nothing could ever again be for her as it had been before. She had the deepest doubts about the point of any philosophizing, a doubt that she never entirely lost. Years later, this also led to her getting caught up in political debates to such an extent that she was expelled from the SED.

When we met in 1997, she said that she couldn't have talked to me about Koestler. "Who knows where I would have ended up if I had talked with you about it," Carla said. And, in fact, I probably would not have borrowed the book from her either. Only after 1989 did I learn that my in-laws had it in their library and that Emanuel also knew the novel. I think now that this political prudence and mistrust, among friends too, and yes, even within one's own family, was a fixed part of the post-Stalinist era's so-called "socialist human community."* Everyone went through the political separation and decision-making process for him- or herself, isolated one from another. Only towards the end of "real existing socialism" did the silence within the much-vaunted community disintegrate, since the political power to which it irrevocably belonged was also disintegrating.

But it was not just within the Institute that I was met with mistrust after I had become a member of the royal household, as Reni called it. I had met Reni at the end of my studies. She was destitute and lived with another woman. She was a lesbian, which was a political crime in the GDR. Reni had also studied philosophy and was having problems with her thesis. Since writing was easier for me and I had fun with her topic on Heine, I helped her. We were good friends in those years. Reni upbraided me severely for having married into the political establishment. She believed that I was thereby lost for all the nobler goals of humanity, among which she also counted Heine's dreams: to establish heaven already on earth. How this heaven could be brought to earth was something that Reni thought about with Heine's texts. But she did not want to write down what she had thought. Forced into words, what she searched the heavens for sounded banal, in her opinion, but with this viewpoint she was not going to be able to complete any thesis. So I wrote down the banalities for her. Thus did Reni succeed in feeling that not she but I had trivialized our longing for a better time through the inadequacy of our language. Reni had a tendency towards brilliant completeness, towards perfection; for that reason, she never finished any project, for something was always missing, and in that regard she was again usually correct.

I caught myself thinking about how, over the years, I became guilty about Reni. Since, with her anarchistic way of life, she was incapable of conforming, she kept herself afloat with occasional work. I started giving Reni money. I offered her clothing. But these gifts left a bitter aftertaste, since financially I was faring better and better. I gave them to her anyway, and she accepted my presents. We both knew that our friendship would be destroyed along with these gifts.

The bitter aftertaste remained. I was reminded of it when, after the Wall fell, I gave money to the beggars and the pedlars. The regarded me just as Reni had, with a reproachful look in their eyes.

8

I reinforced my hideout and withdrew into academic philosophy. I became a Hegel specialist and used my privileged status to avoid having to make a career out of it. I stubbornly rebuffed all political functions and was not penalized for it. Again and again people tried to entice me into a career. If nothing else, with the temptation of joining the "travel cadre" (*Reisekader*). To be part of this group was a privilege, and not just for academics. It consisted only of those people deemed politically reliable enough to represent with dignity and pride the "socialist fatherland – East Germany" abroad in the non-socialist world. The status of *Reisekader* also meant that "comrades" would have trusted me, first, not to stay in the West, and second, to make the proper reports on my travels in the West to the authorities. I told my "comrades," however, that I was not prepared to provide information about the discussions I had with colleagues and friends at conferences or keep a record of such things, which, as required, the Institute would have to make available to the Stasi. I turned down the offer twice and, apart from the fact that I was not allowed to travel, my decision had no further negative consequences. I was left in peace.

This peace was also a result of my social learning process. I had acquired a certain degree of cynicism, which made friendly and formal interactions with my philosophy colleagues possible. Without this cynicism, I could never have managed. Indeed, every co-worker knew that the number of Stasi informants was especially large at such an Institute. But no one knew whether the colleague with whom you had just spoken was harmless or only pretended to be harmless in order to inform on you, or even whether he was spying on the informers' own undercover work. For both the individual and the collective, this situation restricted considerably the sense of peace and comfort and made scholarly work impossible, as I later had to acknowledge.

The best functionaries, and likely not just in the Institute for Philosophy, were paranoid characters. The more pronounced a comrade's persecution complex, the more watchful he or she was, the greater his or her commitment to resisting the internal and the external enemy. This meant that all philosophical books and texts, including the manuscripts of colleagues and comrades, were read and examined for deviations from Marxism-Leninism. Every comrade scholar knew about this and, hence, took precautions when composing his or her texts. These safeguards influenced how sentences were constructed, since it was necessary to write in such a fashion that no revisionism or any other "ism" could be detected in the text as an ideological deviation. The results were hermetically closed tracts or clichéd rehashings of the prevailing Party jargon.

The peace was a cynical peace; that is, pretty much everyone behaved in front of their peers as if they took the required political assemblies seriously. For example, every third Monday everyone met from 3:00 to 5:00 in the afternoon for the trade union meeting. So, during these two hours everyone played "trade union meeting," say on the topic "The Importance of the Collective for Increasing Labour Productivity." Hardly anyone believed the nonsense, but almost everyone played along and helped make the meeting a success by contributing to the discussion. Not only did the time pass more quickly this way, but the meeting would be in order as to its content. This meant that when the meeting was later evaluated there would not be any unpleasantness – for instance, because it had not gone well politically. As the two hours approached their end, the meeting was brought to a close. You then avoided your colleagues again until the next time. If the next time happened to coincide with an official Institute outing, you were covered because you were obliged to attend. Mostly on such trips I did not do anything more than what I usually did. I talked with Carla about theory construction and theories of contradiction, only now I was also wandering through the forest or riding a steamship, and, once we arrived at our destination, instead of eating Carla's excellent potato fritters, we had cutlets or curry sausages on the Institute's dime, chasing it all down with free beer.

This pragmatic way of dealing with the formalities of life at the Academy also extended to the rules of the game for remaining "calm" within the well of Hegel experts. Making formal declarations of faith in Marxism-Leninism was essential to them. So while I could bring to light one subtlety in Hegel after another, I was required to adhere strictly to the citations; that is, I had to prove that the prophets Marx, Engels, and Lenin understood Hegel better than Hegel himself did. Above all it was essential here not to underestimate Lenin's importance. At some point I hit upon the optimal ratio for the citations; after that I did not hear any more complaints: for every five Marx citations, one from Lenin. So I counted up the citations in the entire text and, afterwards, inserted into the footnotes appropriate references from my note card box of "Lenin citations on Hegel."

The question that I asked myself more intently with every year was: how many concessions were necessary for the sake of "pure theory"? How many lies must be told, how much had to be staged to secure a bit of breathing space where one could pursue so-called pure research apart from all the ideological clatter?

When I asked her about the stages of cynicism, Carla understood very well what I was talking about and she reasoned with me. She tried to explain to me the difference between essential and non-essential compromises and between lies and lies. And she still believed that she could outwit the state of affairs.

So I played the game – to conform, not to conform, to conform by not conforming – in order to create free space for myself and be able to leave everything else as it was. To stage sham activities in order to give the impression of political interest. To control oneself emotionally during this game so as not to offer up additional targets, something at which I ultimately did not succeed.

Years passed, however, before I understood that I was actively wearing myself out and stifling my creativity with these tactical games and compromises. In retrospect, it is clear to me that the Philosophical Institute at the Academy went under without any fanfare at all precisely because, in the end, the goal of all its philosophizing was to secure politically the prevailing doctrine of state. Once the GDR collapsed, this philosophy lost its ideological function. It had never had its own philosophical purpose.

At some point in time, those who worked at the Institute discovered that it was most convenient not to express any thoughts at all, to the degree that they even had thoughts. If there were not any of one's own thoughts in the texts that had been submitted, there would be no need to cover oneself. Consequently, the whole business of burying one's own ideas in the holy dogma of Marxism-Leninism so one's independent thought remained politically unsuspicious did not have to take place. Hence, for the humanists and social scientists on staff it was wisest to give up thinking altogether.

9

It was more difficult to reach an agreement with Emanuel about political compromises and the opportunism they required than with Carla or even Reni. His faith was of another consistency. Emanuel did not think about scholarship, he thought about socialism. Despite its many shortcomings, he was utterly convinced that the GDR was the better, the hope-filled future. For him, scholarship was only a second- or even third-rate concern. In first place stood defending and constructing socialism with the same colours with which Gorbachev would later paint them. Emanuel had political dimensions in his head. Scholarship was there to strengthen socialism. What ran counter to this goal was either not thought about or studiously swept aside.

For the time being, Emanuel and I had hopes. We loved each other. Emanuel believed that I would soon understand that socialism was the better form of society for me too. I hoped that, with time, Emanuel would see that, for all its relentless struggles, true happiness was not possible in the socialist human community.

After a certain point in the day I found again that his political standpoint really did not matter to me, so long as he did not force it on me, which he never did. I wanted nothing to do with politics. Ultimately we both avoided political discussions.

Despite all the political differences, it was also possible to interact with Emanuel's family in a friendly manner. The family accepted that I was not of sound mind politically, as they put it, with the best of intentions. The role of the political "dummy" had its advantages, especially since, apart from politics, my father-in-law regarded me as intelligent and lovable. And the rest of the family adopted his position as the value judgment that should prevail.

Beyond the family value, there soon existed a secret between me and my father-in-law. For not long after I began to attend the family gatherings regularly, I presented him with a poem for his birthday. It began: "Evenings the clown cries, almost blinded by the spotlights / he finds in the light of day / no passable paths, / alone on rails of cloud / he tries to slink through the city / but chains of mirrors everywhere / …"* Jürgen Kucyznski read the poem all the way through. Then he said sadly: "You know, my child, a family needs magic. Without magic a family can't function. So let's leave it be. The poem will be our secret. I'll put it in the safe at once. Agreed?" I did agree and from that hour on had the greatest sympathy for him. It sufficed that he knew, and I now knew that he knew.

Even though I did not really understand what a family's magic was, my mother-in-law's concern for me was genuine. I had told her that I was dependent on prescriptions, tended towards panic attacks, and took large quantities of antidepressants before the days I was required to be at the Academy so that I could function properly at the Institute. And that meant: preventing any sort of spontaneity or thoughtless word in order to stay "calm." She knew that I had increased the dosage for the tranquillizers and had become more and more resistant to them.

At some point, she brought me to a behavioural physiologist in the middle of East Berlin for counselling sessions that she paid for, unbeknownst to me. I discovered this when I noticed a letter in my mother-in-law's handwriting on the doctor's desk and, being alone in the room, could not stop myself from reading it. Among other things, the letter requested: "Please don't tell Rita anything about our arrangements. It would only put a strain on her." That was my mother-in-law's genteel discretion, which consistently impressed me. So, during an anti-anxiety training, I learned to fight my fear by countering its neurophysiological stimuli. The family was also kept informed about my success with this therapy. I learned various breathing techniques, including some from the realm of yoga, in order to acquire control over my aggressions and fears. At first I practised this breathing in the therapist's private office, then during the days I had to be at the Institute, keeping a log of the technique and how much time elapsed until the chosen technique produced an effect – or not. After weeks I had my first successes: the breathing techniques were reducing the period between anxiety-stimulus and calming. Soon I was sitting anxiety-free and relaxed in Institute and Party meetings and wrote poetry. I learned to tune out most of what went on during these rather meaningless meetings, reacting only when my name was mentioned. I gained the reputation of having become more mature.

Reni commented on my training against anxiety attacks with the sentence: "If you want to let yourself be trained à la Pavlov to be a political monkey who learns how to react without emotion when he hears catchphrases like 'secret police' or 'Party secretary,' then you must do it. Long live love!" Now and then, she also said that I was dependent on Emanuel. But that was nonsense.

For the first time after ten years of forced existence in East Germany, Emanuel and his family gave me the opportunity for a recovery period. Protected by the family, which stood by me unfailingly, I could finally let myself go a bit. I was no longer alone in this land.

Once more I was moving between two extremes. It had long ago become my life to exist in at least two worlds. The transition from one extreme to the other was a familiar habit to me. Leading life in such different worlds that they did not touch each other. Taking care so that the one world could not break into the other. In short, avoiding chaos so as not to lose again the little bit of orientation I had acquired. For the fear of losing my mind in the span between the extremes was still there. It awoke at night, the fear, and approached me. But now Emanuel slept there next to me. Often the movement of his hand over my head sufficed to suffocate the anxiety.

That the relationship between Emanuel and myself lasted twenty years – with all the ups and downs that, for better or worse, go along with a marriage that was lived in an essentially bourgeois fashion – stemmed above all, for my part, from the sense of security that Emanuel exuded. He had been raised in the certainty that the world belonged to him. He had grown up in bourgeois tranquillity, intellectual self-confidence, and the real advantages that naturally prevailed, so to speak, in his parents' house.

I soon understood that Emanuel was also a hero-child and, like Esther, lived in a world that had nothing to do with the existence of the vast majority of his fellow citizens. He, too, possessed the unworldliness that I had so liked in the antifa-kids from my school year. Unlike Esther, he did not sing any Jewish songs. But he could tell Jewish jokes for hours and their punch lines pleased me. He believed in himself and in the future, which naturally belonged to him; he believed in his mission as a child of antifascist-communist parents. He wanted to contribute to the success of the world revolution by putting his life in its service. He was also a true child of the Party, which he loved and regarded as part of his greater family. He was proud of East Germany, the first Workers' and Peasants' State. His eyes shone when he spoke about the future, about the elimination of any sort of oppression or exploitation. His belief in socialism, in whose realization he was fortunate enough to be able to participate, was genuine.

But genuine too was his conviction that he had been "chosen" and thus had to assume the lead in the struggle for a better world. Just like Esther and the other hero-children, he had no doubt about his duty as the child of "history's victors" to become a leader in this struggle. This duty appeared as his inheritance, transferred from parents to son. Seen in this way, for Emanuel, his later career as a member of the nomenklatura was more a sacrifice for the "greater good of humanity" than a career, which increased his privileged status in the GDR immensely. This aloofness and unworldliness, which could also be useful, he shared with many other of the antifascist children. These qualities made his life go smoothly and soon mine too, since I never discussed his sense of being chosen with him. But that does not mean that the self-confidence with which he accepted it did not make me aggressive.

Our compromise notwithstanding, Emanuel's self-confidence and belief did me good. His unshakeable optimism was the counterweight to the hopelessness that remained my only constant since the collapse of my musical life. It was important to me that Emanuel believed so strongly. Had he believed in the Virgin Mary with the same intensity as he did in socialism, for his sake I would have gone with him to midnight Mass at Christmas instead of the May Day rallies.

I suppressed the irrational part of his belief in and his relationship to the Party. Only reluctantly did I comprehend that, in critical situations, he would always decide in favour of the Party. The Party was his "Holy Spirit" whose perfection neither I nor our love could reach, whose perfection nothing and no one could reach. And "the Party" had to be defended, no matter the cost. This part of his Stalinist upbringing and its hardness towards humanity I feared.

As long as it worked out, and over the years it worked out for us increasingly well, we arranged our life together chiefly around scholarly work. We tried to keep our daily life free from "actual" work. As far as possible, anything that could disturb our scholarship either did not take place or occurred using the least amount of time and energy. Good working conditions were a priority. In our own way, we lived a spartan existence in East Germany. We had no car, no garden, no house, no boat. All this would have taken up valuable time in the GDR: time to find craftsmen, acquire replacement parts, maintain the necessary relations for purchases and exchanges. All of this would have kept us from our "real" work. We did not have children, since I did not want to bring any into this world. I did not want to be guilty for their existence. I knew that I would not be able to offer them anything but unhappiness for their unhappiness. That they could be happy, just like that, was beyond my power of imagination. I was afraid of having my own children, too, because I was afraid of the question with which I had pestered my mother: the reproachful question of why she had brought me into the world. Over the years, Emanuel had come to terms with my position. I had told him rather early on and well before we had married that if he wanted children I was not the wife for him.

The one thing we did have was books, more than there was room for in the apartment. And we always had domestic help, who guaranteed that the house had a minimal degree of order.

My mother-in-law managed to find me a psychotherapist in East Berlin who combined psychoanalysis – which was taboo in East Germany – with behavioural therapy. Soon I was going to private sessions with an analyst. He was an émigré from Chile and came to East Berlin after the Allende regime was overthrown.* As a psychoanalyst he was not officially allowed to work, since psychoanalysis along with Sigmund Freund was an invention of the imperialist class enemy. However, he could treat some patients privately. I spent more than three years on his couch, connecting and tying threads that had either split or that I myself had cut.

At last I found my way into the life that should become mine. At some point, the family meals tasted good to me. I stopped protesting and excusing myself. I understood that all attempts at explanation were pointless and only made matters worse. I accustomed myself to having lunch with the family in the East German government's restaurants, since my mother-in-law had too much work with all the guests who came to Berlin, especially in the summer. They were mostly Marxist intellectuals from the United States, England, and Australia, who took advantage of their summer breaks to travel in Europe. I listened to what they related and learned something about the outside world that was not accessible to me. So much English was spoken then that I learned to understand it passively.

I grew used to meeting ministers and state civil servants even during these family meals at the government restaurants, where they greeted me courteously as a member of the family and gave us tips on which of the set menus was the best that day. At the time, I knew a poet named Emmi. She was having an affair with one of the deputy ministers of culture and the affair was well known. The deputy minister often arranged to meet us when the family ate together on Sundays in the government hotel "Johannishof."* When he greeted me, every now and then he would slip me letters for Emmi so that they did not fall into the hands of the Stasi before the beloved had read them.

I accepted the role of playing a Kuczynski and, accordingly, had clothes made for me. I had my own style, characterized by lightweight, dark wools, silk, and chiffon, in which I could hide myself. This style was later imitated within the Academy. I wore my grandmother's jewellery and changed how I walked. I remembered the bourgeois part of my upbringing and learned from my mother-in-law how to make French sauces and cook plum pudding. Emanuel was pleased with me.

10

Outside the games I had to play to adapt to my privileged existence – that is, out in the real existing GDR – frustration with the mendacity of the new regime, now led by Honecker, was growing. The frustration came primarily from East German citizens for whom the change in power had given rise to hope that, through honesty and hard work, a more reasonable way could still be found to enable the construction of a new, a better socialist world. Among their singers was Wolf Biermann, who unsparingly sang out his criticism of the politbureaucracy.* Because he believed in communism, his songs possessed a candour and roguish earnestness that sang directly to the heart.

When Wolf Biermann was stripped of his citizenship in 1976, I was outraged and began to protest at the top of my voice, and not just in the Academy. One just didn't do something like that. A country that can't tolerate its singers, I argued, is at an end. Then I began to feel the family's full force. Emanuel implored me not to sign any sort of protest letter and sought cover for his arguments within the family. My father-in-law, who was himself shocked by Biermann's expulsion and described it as "stupidity" within the family, warned me in a paternally authoritarian manner not to take part in any kind of protest action. I could not take a stand against the Party, he said. The Party was always right,* even when it was wrong, was his opportunistic reasoning – with which he himself survived all of East Germany's political crises. He urgently advised me to follow this ideological formula now. Because I could not observe it, my mother-in-law suggested that for now I should drop out of sight by calling in sick. The family would be grateful for it. Moreover, it would be in Emanuel's interest. I was too weak to offer any resistance. But I knew that I had exceeded the limit of my willingness to compromise. I knew that I would not recover from this concession. I would not be able to continue as before.

For the first time, I found myself confronted with the political consequences of what it meant to play a Kuczynski. The role in which I had just been coached came back to me and showed me the logic of the game in which I had got mixed up. The family's power, which normally kept me free from everyday political squabbling, had, in this critical situation, dragged me irrevocably into the political divorce proceedings between citizens loyal to the state and citizens in the "critical opposition." Unexpectedly, I found myself again on the side of the reliable state servants who were true to the Party line. Whereas Biermann and, later, other opponents of the regime were stripped of their citizenship and expelled from East Germany, and whereas other critical citizens withdrew from official GDR politics, I was dragged into them and found myself again on the side of the political establishment. I suddenly functioned as a Kuczynski family member and carried on the family business. I felt as if I had been blackmailed, blackmailed because of my desire not to lose the family's affections. Had I protested in public, that would have meant breaking with the family, where for the first time in the GDR I felt secure. Neither Emanuel nor his parents would have made allowances for me. An unyielding commitment to Party discipline was one of the foundations of their belief, it was part of the higher cause that the godlike Party was for them. And no worldly or logical argument could ever be made against it.

While my public silence about Biermann's loss of citizenship prevented a break with the family, inwardly I began distancing myself from the family. The result of my having to call in sick for weeks was my resolution never to be blackmailed like that again. So while outwardly I behaved like a member of the family, thereafter I distanced myself emotionally – first from the family and then later from Emanuel.

The revocation of Biermann's citizenship led to a polarization between dogmatic and opposition-minded intellectuals. Written protests from artists opposing Biermann's expulsion increased. This was the first time that prominent East Germans had protested publicly since the Warsaw Pact countries' invasion of Czechoslovakia. Correspondingly unyielding was the SED leadership's reaction to the recent efforts to discuss the problems of socialism within a democratic public sphere. The dialogue between the critical intellectuals and the Party leadership broke off. Where criticism could not be prevented, reprisals were launched. I was more isolated than before and thrown back on the family.

Four weeks after Wolf Biermann's citizenship was revoked, I defended my dissertation – another reason why I ultimately kept quiet. I knew all too well that I would never have received my degree if I had been openly involved in the protest. I had been provocative enough with what I had already said. I defended my dissertation and knew that it wouldn't have any further meaning for me.

I thought about what I could do to disappear from my philosophical life. Cautiously, I spoke with Emanuel about it. Predictably, he didn't think much of my ideas. I knew, too, that he wouldn't like at all my idea of at last leaving East Germany, say, for my sake. I knew that I didn't stand a chance.

I talked it over with Reni. She was still unemployed, and thus officially considered "antisocial," and alarmingly depressive. Carla, however, was ready to help. Together we managed to obtain a position for Reni at the Institute for Philosophy. Reni had hit bottom, to the point that she didn't protest even once. I didn't know at the time that Reni was not only playing with the idea of leaving East Germany but was also well along with her plans to flee. One day, after she had regained her composure somewhat at the Institute, Reni introduced me to a man. He was a Swiss guy named Hans. Reni said that she loved him and intended to marry him. I looked at Hans and then at Reni. She was a lesbian through and through. When we were alone I told her that the man was not someone who smuggled people across borders – he was a Stasi informant. She should stay away from him and never again bring him to my place. Over the years, I had developed a good ear for detecting informants. I could rely on my ear. Reni didn't believe me. Half a year later Reni's partner gave me the news that Reni had been arrested for trying to flee the Republic.

Since she had vouched for Reni, the Stasi interrogated Carla. I was not questioned even once. Someone had kept me clear from the investigation, as a Kuczynski family member. Emanuel told me firmly and clearly that if I ever visited Reni in prison that would be the end of our relationship in every respect. I did not go, but my relationship to Emanuel changed. A bit of my love for him had been irreparably shattered. I began to calculate the costs of our relationship.

Reni sat in jail for almost a year before she was ransomed and sent to West Germany.* At the time I was working on the third version of an article for an international anthology on Hegel. Since there was still a thought in it that did not seem properly supported by references to Marx or Lenin, it was returned to me. I rewrote the article so thoroughly that it never came back again. Instead I was praised for finally understanding the criticism. Then the article appeared in a volume cynically titled *On the Courage of Understanding*. Out of self-respect, I knew I could never allow something like that to happen again. My hideout in Hegelian philosophy had proven to be a fallacy.

To mark the upcoming sesquicentennial of Hegel's death in 1981, I received the honourable commission of writing a biography of Hegel, which had been sent to the Institute from the Central Committee of the SED. It figured among the most important assignments planned for the Institute for Philosophy in the 1978/9 academic year. I began by reviewing the literature and wrote. I wrote according to how I imagined that a Hegel biography should be written. I cut myself off from all the censorship nonsense. Then suddenly and unexpectedly there was once more a melody in me; I had to pursue it. It organized the facts about Hegel in its own way, and mixed the facts with metaphors into a text that surprised me and each day surprised me anew. The whole thing was very exciting. I wrote and wrote. Hegel became a medium in which I found my language again: "Philosophy begins where a break has occurred with the actual world and its life. Philosophy is the expression of one's diremption from real life." This insight of Hegel's became the background music for my text. It corresponded to my own experiences with philosophy. I searched for sentences and reasons for myself and at last found words that again belonged to me. I had not expected that amidst the theories and philosophies I could return to myself. There was a melody, right in the middle of this edifice of categories. It had its own dynamic and a tune that altered the structure of the theoretical spaces. And all at once, the path I had travelled only to return to myself in the end seemed immeasurably long. I played with the words as I previously played with notes. I wanted them to ring, the categories. I was in the process of connecting my experience with philosophy – and the reason for studying it excessively – to my previous life.

I recalled that, as a pianist, I could never make up my mind about whether the piano was made for the purpose of performance or for free improvisation and composition. My long-forgotten urge to produce my own individual creations had thus found a new, a literary outlet. That remained the most important result of the analysis: It dawned on me that I was still an artist, however much I had fought against it for all those years.

This insight created its own path for itself; inexorably it pulled me out of the thicket of philosophies. What I had written was still foreign to me, since I was hearing from myself again for the first time in years. I knew that what I was writing was not what the comrades in the SED's Central Committee would let pass as a Hegel biography. But I was in agreement with myself about it and ready to bear the consequences.

It astonished me that just at this moment, now that I had long ago said goodbye to my existence as a professional philosopher and was pursuing my own "text" alone, I was reputed at the Institute to have become reasonable. In that year alone I received two raises, even though I had not produced anything new at all.

Only years later did I understand that I was being offered hush money, precisely because I had so revised the article on Hegel that it was no longer possible to find any of my own thoughts in it. I was also honoured at the time by being allowed to attend a major philosophy conference at the Palace of the Republic.* Since I had never before been approved for such a venerable conference, I underwent a security screening and then received the yellow card. This meant that I was allowed to sit in the outer security circle when Politburo member Kurt Hager appeared at the conference to pour out his wisdom on the heads of three hundred philosophers.* Sitting at an appropriate distance from the GDR's chief philosopher for security reasons, I heard again that objectively there was no alienation in East Germany and that this was a Party decision from the highest level. The philosophers assembled at the Palace of the Republic were urged to explain precisely this Politburo decision philosophically and propagandistically in order to put an immediate stop to the public discussion of alienation. In the outer security circle and at the greatest distance from Politburo member Kurt Hager, I doodled flowers on the yellow security card and said goodbye once and for all to philosophy as it was practised in the GDR.

At this very moment, a huge political scandal hit the Institute for Philosophy. Carla and a few other philosophers, who were still labouring on their theories, had the brave idea of fighting for a theoretical application of philosophy in the Institute. That would mean ousting the Institute's administration, namely by the power of the spirit. The whole thing sounded pretty risky in light of the Party line that had just been adopted.

But Carla was head over heels in love with a talented theorist, who had not been at the Institute very long. Together with him she wanted to bring theoretical philosophy to bear at last. With her little Hans, she intended to instal philosophy as a science and revolutionize the Institute. I asked which member of the Politburo was backing them, asked whether they had received the assignment to overthrow the Institute directly from Honecker, given the rubbish that Hager had just let loose at the philosophy conference. When I learned that no one was behind them – apart from a few virtuous comrades from the new West German Communist Party (and they had been suspended as members in the now banned Communist Party of Germany)* and from the SED in West Berlin – I broke out into one of the fits of laughter for which I was well known. I hadn't expected so much unworldliness even from professional philosophers. I understood that Carla was in love. But I begged her to realize that while her little Hans was indeed clever and likeable, I didn't want to give up my life for him. I would understand, though, if she gave up hers. However, I wanted to determine for myself how I left philosophy.

So I arranged to take sick leave once more, this time with the help of a psychiatrist at Charité Hospital. I was friends with him. In East Germany, a doctor specializing in mental illness and emotional disorders could be an institution that lay beyond all political assessments. When such a doctor said I was sick, no one from either the Institute or the Party leadership could harass me to make political statements. A psychiatrist could pull me out of the political maelstrom without himself risking political persecution. Together we came up with a diagnosis, created an appropriate medical report, and back-dated it by two years. Then he gave me directions on how to behave. He prescribed antidepressants for me, which I was not supposed to take and did not. Since he was the frugal type, he asked me to bring the pills – which for security reasons I should pick up at the pharmacy – along with me to my checkups. In this way I ended up on sick leave for five months, namely on account of reactive depression. The doctor for mental illness and emotional disorders advised me to break out in tears whenever I heard the words "Institute for Philosophy" in official settings. Thus, when summoned to the Medical Control Commission, I played the part of one clinically depressed, which was not particularly difficult for me.

The insurrection of spirit against power was crushed by the SED Central Committee and the Berlin district leadership. Carla and her little Hans were expelled from the Party, and either fired from the Institute or transferred for disciplinary reasons.

After all the political hoopla had subsided somewhat, I resigned from the Institute by mutual agreement with the administration. Had I left the Academy at the same time that all the firings and disciplinary actions were being carried out at the Institute, my resignation would have been associated with the ongoing wave of ideological purges. My father-in-law reasoned with me in the strongest terms to wait several months before giving notice. After all, he asked, didn't I wanted to have my book on Hegel published in East Germany? Or not? I did want it, for I didn't want to lose Emanuel. And the GDR and its politics were still not so important to me that, for their sake, I would bring about a major falling-out with the family. Indeed, my principle of hopelessness, which I lived in the GDR, arose from the very realization that it was senseless to let oneself be used up for this vision of a socialist future.

What struck me from my Kuczynski-niche, in these years when opposition to the regime was being expressed, were the different ways it was dealt with. If the opposition figures were nameless, they were treated harshly because they were defenceless. When they were deported after serving their prison sentences, they often did not take with them anything more than what they were wearing when they were released. If the opposition members came from the GDR's more privileged ranks, if they were artists who had already received the National Order of Merit and the National Prize from the East German government for their successful work towards the construction of a socialist homeland, the Party leadership handled them more carefully. After endless conversations and attempts at reconciliation, they were usually allowed to leave the country peacefully. They could also take their cats and dogs with them as long as they had valid vaccination certificates. In the 1980s, they could occasionally even keep their apartments, at least those in East Berlin. The carefully dispensed privileges applied here too.

In any case, family members of East German VIPs and the nomenklatura had their own special file boxes at the Stasi offices and were also judged by different standards. In that respect, I not only lived a highly privileged life, I also had a privileged Stasi file. Someone once called to my attention that as a "member" my file was stored with those of other "members" in a special department. My files were never taken out of this special card file for privileged cadres and their dependants; they could only be moved more to the front or to the back according to my behaviour.

I thus wished to stay in East Germany. Despite all the differences of opinion, I felt comfortable in the family that helped me when I could be helped. I learned to appreciate it, precisely because I myself never had a family that could protect me. I was grateful to the family, especially my father-in-law, who always defended me – even within the family – and who, above all, loved my intellectual irreverence. I didn't read most of his books, since I couldn't cope with them politically. He did not read any of my books, apart from my book on Hegel, because he found my writing too gloomy. More importantly, we had great affection for one another, which was also the cause of some envy within the family.

Since I wanted to publish my book on Hegel in East Germany, I had to bear in mind that the wife of my, by then, all-powerful Institute head worked in the Ministry of Culture, Censorship Division, and was responsible for all proceedings to authorize the publication of philosophical works in East Germany. I was well aware of that basic fact. But only then did I understand that something like a family business had come into existence there. Had I left the Academy of Sciences during the political ruckus earlier, I would not have been able to publish my Hegel book in East Germany.

This was hardly a paranoid fantasy. The family business ran smoothly. After my book had sat for a year and a half in the central office for publication licences in the Ministry of Culture, I received a phone call one morning from the wife of my former boss. She said she found my book to be really good and even intelligible. Therefore she would approve its publication.

The book was published in an edition of four thousand copies for the East German market, where, in this self-styled "country of readers," print runs of umpteen thousand copies were not unusual. One-third of my copies went into the collections of the National People's Army; the rest were released for sale. With this strategy of a very limited edition and using the Army as a distribution point, two problems were solved at once. First, a Kuczynski was not banned professionally; second, the book was hardly available in the stores. There were effectively no reviews of the book. A new edition also never materialized. Licensing arrangements to sell the book in West Germany were also successfully blocked by the officials responsible for security affairs in the Ministry of Culture.

After reunification, I picked up a few copies of my Hegel book from the Army libraries, since I hardly had any myself.

Ten years of being a specialist: In my head, I had learned to survive. I had learned to provide answers to every question and construct universal propositions, that is statements that are correct from front to back and from back to front, which could enjoy the acclaim of professionals in the field. I had learned to conceal myself behind rational sentences. I had learned to speak the universal language. Out of my own fear of fear,

I had become a specialist in the universal. By my own choice, I reduced myself to the bare essentials, the necessary generalities. Indeed, the world was remote. No shouting. No thorn bush that burned. No small light. No voice against another voice. The law of the world lay silently over everything so that I myself seemed innocent of my well-knit lies. I have lived extremely far away from myself and learned to lie as part of the collective. I have tried out the cynic's way of life and could not endure it.

Ultimately I understood that I could not outwit the circumstances, even using the cunning of reason.

I understood the compulsiveness of deductive thinking. I have lived the phantasm of logical consistency, which was supposed to reveal "world," independent of any experience of reality. I built myself a fictional world. As a paradox within a paradox, I succeeded in using the "revolutionary method" to shutter my world off from any actual world.

To live contrary to experience, that too I have learned from this philosophy. To close one's eyes and say that nothing at all has happened, even though everything has already happened.

II

Disguising myself as a housewife worked well. No one took me seriously, especially not politically. When at all, people took note of me only as a member of the Kuczynski family, and that is how I appeared in official records.

Emanuel, meanwhile, was about to launch his career in the ranks of nomenklatura. Over the years he had been groomed to follow in his father's footsteps as an economist and a historian. To this end he first took over the Institute of Economic History at the Academy. His father had founded it and achieved for it a certain international reputation. Emanuel thought it entirely normal that the father would pass the Institute torch on to the son so that he could carry on what the father had started. After all, and this was also the family consensus, they were both fighting for the good of the people and for socialist science. At the same time, they were both devoted to the Party. From year to year, Emanuel became more important socially. As the child of immigrants from England he spoke English quite well, which was rare in East Germany, and for that reason was also chosen to serve on countless international commissions. He believed in his special responsibility as a hero-child and thus agreed to devote all his energy to building a better world.

I didn't discuss this with him, inventing instead a life to go with his. On the advice of my mother-in-law, I took care of things at the tailor, where my father-in-law had been having his suits made for years. I selected the fabrics and colours for Emanuel's many suits and picked out his ties. My in-laws were grateful for my cares; after all, Emanuel had to make the right impression. He even started to receive an allowance now to cover such "image-related" expenses. I practised my part of being the housewife and partner of an increasingly important man within the intellectual nomenklatura. I imitated my mother-in-law, to the entire family's relief. That I was well brought up, didn't talk nonsense at receptions, and could offer guests a good home-cooked meal fully fitted this role. Just as it did that I had both a general and specific knowledge of literature, music, and philosophy and could charm guests from "capitalist foreign countries" with it. For a while, I actually had a lot of fun with my invented life as a married woman. I had always had fun when there was something to play and took pains to play the piece as well as I could. That was something I had learned at the piano – as well as changing quickly from one piece to another.

I was outside of everything. Or better. I was fully in the middle. Had I wanted to get further out, I would also have had to leave East Germany physically. For there really was nothing left in my life that had anything to do with normal life in East Germany. My last, already dubious tie with the GDR, the Philosophical Institute at the Academy, lay behind me. Before me lay life in the gardens of the nomenklatura. From its trees I could observe the important goings-on of the country's political and academic elite, and that is what I did.

Within the inner circle of the political and academic nomenklatura, people held parties and celebrated anniversaries as they arose, and took delight in the economy's apparent successes, which, in fact, resulted from the billions in West German government loans that flowed into the country and substantially delayed the GDR from going bankrupt. Of course, as part of the Kuczynski family, I attended such festivities.

At the Kuczynski house, the most important celebrations occurred every five years in honour of my father-in-law's birthday. Every five years they became more pompous, and the line of people offering their congratulations grew longer and longer. My father-in-law had a thoroughly ironic attitude towards the official circus. But he was also always flattered when Politburo members appeared and even praised him.

Following Honecker's rise to power, my father-in-law had become his ghost writer on matters concerning the capitalist world economy, and he was extremely proud that Honecker was almost the only Party leader in the socialist world who said something now and then about the world economy, and something clever at that. Since the general secretary's words on the world economy couldn't be repeated often enough, after the content of Honecker's speech at this plenary session of the SED or that Party conference had become known, Jürgen Kuczynski wrote an article for the Party paper, *Neues Deutschland* (New

Germany), about the part of the speech he had composed. That meant, he welcomed the considerable insight into the state of the capitalist world economy that Honecker had most recently offered. At the same time, he stressed or downplayed this or that part of the speech, so that "the people" could understand better what mattered in the capitalist world economy.

As international recognition for East Germany and the West's satisfaction with Honecker grew, Jürgen Kuczynski's political importance also grew. The importance of his birthday likewise grew despite the ebb and flow of disgruntlement within the Politburo towards this or that statement or view. About the antagonistic contradictions in socialism, for instance, which, by definition, did not exist. The line of those wanting to congratulate him grew longer. And almost everyone in the family associated the sea of flowers on the second floor of the house rather with a funeral that had got out of control. Hence, after such a birthday party, my mother-in-law asked all the children to take as many flowers home with them as they could carry.

For these state birthdays, the streets along the official route that members of the Politburo and the SED's Central Committee would take to attend the celebration were swept clean. Then, three to four hours before the state visit, inconspicuous men in dark green and blue cloaks "made in East Germany" spread through the streets. Most of them carried a folding umbrella. Parked cars with drivers stood on the side streets and at the intersections. This scenario for securing the leader of the state from his people was well-known throughout the country. When I turned into Parkstrasse hours before the reception to help my mother-in-law with the final preparations, the sentries greeted me. I did not return their greeting. As part of the family, I could get away with that – and not just on this day – before disappearing behind the green garden gate. The unobtrusive men played with their walkie-talkies and tested their range, visibly pleased with the new technology deployed in the battle to secure the safety of the coming well-wishers.

At just such a birthday party, Günter Mittag, a Politburo member,* once appeared, and I learned the state secret that Mr Mittag had a wooden leg. Or perhaps even two? I don't know any more. It impressed me, though, that this fact was a state secret into which I had now been initiated as part of the family.

As a spouse, on such birthdays I walked through the second floor of the house on Parkstrasse, with its fourteen rooms, all full of books, and every now and then replenished the champagne. In my daytime role as a family member, I chatted about the latest news and fashions. On the face of it, it might seem inconsistent that in making the rounds I found it satisfying to speak casually with the reigning orthodoxy. In such moments I had observed myself and noticed how my fear diminished, since at times like these I felt that nothing could happen to me. How I ever could have forgotten that pretty much everything had already happened to me, I do not know. Why I needed the illusion that I was doing quite well, why I sought encouragement for this fixed idea from, of all people, the country's reigning politbureaucracy, was certainly grounded in the fear that was always still there, when I admitted it. Then it stood enormous before me, so that I could no longer put one foot in front of the other. With the fear came that sadness, which it was better not to allow anymore. At least, that was what I had intended. For this sadness could soon mix up all my daytime roles and suddenly raise the question: what is the point of this entire act? I did not want it to get that far, for I had decided that all lamentations were in vain. I played along and positioned myself between me and myself. I played for the small bit of free space that I had set up for myself in the trees.

This sort of birthday court was staged according to a strict hierarchy. Coming to congratulate Jürgen Kuczynski and, at the same time, to see and be seen were representatives first from the Politburo, then the secretaries of the SED Central Committee, the presidents of the Academy, the Party district secretaries, and the secretaries of the Writers' Association, down to the National Front and the Women's Association. Honecker himself never came to such an affair. But when a member of the Politburo showed up, especially one who was currently in high standing, it was clear that Jürgen Kuczynski had not fallen out of favour with Honecker's Politburo.

My father-in-law himself adopted this phrase – "I have fallen out of favour again" – for the memoirs he published in 1992. For a member of the academic nomenklatura, to fall out of favour meant that you had made some sort of political statement that had angered a Politburo member. To be in or out of favour and to claim that antagonistic contradictions existed under socialism, or even alienation, was something that just was not allowed. The struggle of the social scientific nomenklatura was thus the struggle between knowledge and the Party line. In between stood Party discipline, which functioned as a regulating agent, and the enormous presumption of deciding what "our people" were allowed to know and what not. The scholarly nomenklatura's struggle was also the struggle over what the Politburo – for its and one's own comfort – should and should not know. It was all about not spoiling the old men's mood.

If the discrepancy between the Party's official pronouncements and visibly poor conditions became so great that there was real danger of unrest among the East German people, then the Party line would have to be moderated. Intellectual authorities were responsible for softening the tone. Had Jürgen Kuczynski not voluntarily returned to East Germany as an antifascist immigrant from England, then the Party would have had to invent him as an authority who possessed certain traits, just as it had done with Stephan Hermlin.* Essential here was the combination of an antifascist, communist, and educated middle-class background in one intellectual. The antifascist and communist elements served as political legitimation and allowed the authority to say more than other intellectuals, while the educated middle-class background linked him to the historical tradition of the revolutionary bourgeoisie that, according to the official propaganda, the GDR had inherited. Both Hermlin and Kuczynski played a mediating function in East Germany between the critical intellectuals and the Party line. Their role was to say what other scholars or writers were not allowed to say. Their close friendship with Erich Honecker was not just symbolic. It was real. The artful aspect of what both men did lay in saying what was allowed, and then a little bit more. This "little bit more" was their political risk, but at the same time their intellectual achievement. In return, they received all sorts of decorations and public commendations, because to deploy and dispense this skill properly also required enormous discipline.

This mediating function between Party leadership and intellectually engaged public increased along with the GDR's growing international acceptance and its rapprochement with the West. On the one hand, there was a demand for dialogue and panel discussions such as those that Stephan Hermlin initiated. Here he proclaimed himself to be a late-bourgeois thinker, but tactically these discussions were also conceived as invitations to Western bourgeois intellectuals. On the other hand, the mediating function increased proportionately as the GDR was nearing its end and as the discrepancy between the poor state of affairs in East Germany and the official announcements became more apparent. The greater the disparity, the greater Jürgen Kuczynski's importance and his role as the people's enlightener, which he performed voluntarily and with utmost seriousness. Enlightenment: the Party and Kuczynski were both fascinated by this magic word. Explaining the inexplicable, stating it word for word. In all this, the passion for enlightenment was always directed towards achieving a political balance between the people and the Party leadership. Jürgen Kuczynski's great impact stemmed from his intellectual worldliness, with which he tried to make people understand that while he indeed understood the people's rage, the "Party" could only have acted as it did in this case. The intellectually interested public gratefully accepted his balancing role as the people's "enlightener," since the inexplicable seemed to have been explained – at least for the moment. People no longer saw themselves left alone with all the many contradictions of political life.

On top of all the privileges that I enjoyed as part of the elite came, unexpectedly, one more. Because a literary press had published my book, *Nächte mit Hegel*, I was now perceived as an author. This surprised me for a number of reasons. It seemed ridiculous to me, but as an author I was accorded a type of social importance that irritated me at first, but at which I later had to laugh. Until the GDR's final days, it was hard for me to take seriously the state's sudden interest in my freelance activities, as they were now called.

I understood quite well the basic reason for this interest: it was a matter of control that was no longer being exerted through the customary institutional channels. I no longer had a boss or a work group, nor was I involved with any work-related Party or union organization.

Soon after my existence as a housewife became known, I was invited to join the Writers' Association. One of the district secretaries asked me if I was satisfied with my apartment, if I needed a car, a vacation, and so on. If I had a problem, I was told, I could come to them any time. I thanked him cordially and left it at that.

Only after the Wall fell in 1989* did I become a member of the Association, since for a short time I had the impression that I would have to take a stand against the literary big shots, precisely because I was better acquainted with their box of demagogic and rational tricks than many of the protesting authors were.

Until my departure from the Academy, I had hardly thought at all about the reasons for the numerous privileges accorded notable East German writers and artists. Only now did I realize their political role. Since only a fictitious public sphere existed in the East German media, as self-employed individuals writers and artists were a personified opportunity either for expressing grievances or for covering them up. They too could assume a mediating function between rulers and ruled in the GDR and were, thus, of enormous political importance. This mediating function could be exercised in two ways. By the critical artists, whose works sought to highlight abuses and shortcomings in order to make them matters of public discussion. Or by the state artists and the court poets, whose works extolled existing conditions under socialism as the happiest ones ever known to humanity. In times of political equilibrium, the critical artists and those who were true to the Party line balanced each other out. They thus contributed to a balancing of interests within the opinion-shaping process supervised by the Party leadership. In times of political tension, however, those artists who saw themselves as propagandists for the reigning orthodoxy gained the upper hand. The content and extent of discussion allowed in the People's State was then determined either by the censorship officials in the Ministry of Culture or by censoring the literary and daily press. The greater the actual difference between the people and state power, the more important for East German citizens were the writers and artists who expressed what everyone knew.

Critical artists and writers who said more than they were allowed were disciplined. When this was not sufficient, campaigns were launched against them. To compel the compliance of a critical writer, the state would revoke some of the carefully calibrated privileges from him. For instance, if in his literary production a writer exceeded what was allowed and said something that, in the context of "freedom of expression," should not have been said, then some of the "extras" he had enjoyed were revoked. He might still be able to travel in the West, but only with a restricted private visa, which unknown or young artists never were allowed to do. Other recognized artists lost their business visas, which allowed them to travel in and out of the country regularly on official GDR business. Still other artists were allowed to maintain foreign-exchange bank accounts, or were told it was no longer allowed. Some were punished by being denied new cars from the special automotive pool that supplied the country's prominent people, having to suffer instead through the normal ten-year waiting period; others were denied a telephone connection. When artists protested in the Western media that they were not allowed to travel to the Frankfurt book fair* to give readings of their works, the politically immature East German citizens were not indignant. The politically immature East German citizens loved their writers. They were grateful that these artists stated what they were not allowed to state. They stuck to their parts in the political role playing. Only once they demanded for themselves what the artists had long been allowed, that is, that the privileges be open to everyone equally, did the GDR collapse.

The more that East German artists had come to an arrangement with the East German political system or believed that their importance was truly based on their talent, that is, on their "work," the harder their loss of political and social status in the new Federal Republic hit them.

Common to all the privileged and even the less privileged East German artists and writers was their belief that socialism was a better future and that they wanted to have a hand in shaping it. Since I lacked this faith, I had no chance of forging an emotional connection with them. I could share neither their anger nor, later, their despair that socialism had not become what they had dreamed it would be. Socialism did not exist in my dreams.

I continued to write but avoided playing the artist's social role. I lacked the intellectual courage to predict what was valid and what should be true. And for a long time I was not certain myself if I really was a writer. Furthermore, I had hung around philosophy for too long. I had understood that our knowledge is primarily a practised ritual that serves to conceal our speechlessness in the face of the real. I had learned that the more clearly we construct our sentences, the less we understand about what actually has happened or is still happening. I lacked the philosophical naïveté with which many East German artists described or invoked the future. After ten years as a historian of philosophy, I lacked the philosophical innocence to believe that I, of all people, should know what has validity and what has the grounding to become truth. Reason, God, the meaning of world history – everything that could be said about them had been said long ago.

I had emigrated to my study. Here was my niche, which I sought to seal off. This is where I would soon become a master of my craft. I invented a hideout within a hideout; in everything I did I found another hideout. I went away without ever having changed my location. Once more, I was not living in the world that surrounded me, I lived in the novel that I had begun to write. In its characters, I tried to encounter myself. I invented life in order to distance myself from life "out there." I pursued a new escape route after I had abandoned the transcendental heights. This was the route back into an artistic existence. Here I could fall back on my experiences. Here, once again, I was only somewhat the creator of my own circumstances.

I secured my financial independence from the state's grants and funding by becoming financially dependent on the family. I came to terms with the compromise of living off the family because, ultimately, I stayed in the background politically for their sake and had only stayed in East Germany because of Emanuel. In addition, the family made it easy for me, for I never heard anyone reproach me for earning hardly anything. At Christmas, in fact, every child received the so-called "Zettelchen," the Christmas cheque. The more my father-in-law published or lectured, the bigger the cheque. He'd rather give while he was still alive, he said. We needed money while we were young. In old age, he commented, one no longer had the strength to spend it. Moreover, we wouldn't rejoice quite so much at his death. And so each year we all looked forward to the Christmas cheque. In addition, Emanuel's own salary rose considerably the more he pursued his work as a member of the nomenklatura. Since we didn't have a house, a garden, or even a car, we had plenty of money, more than we could ever spend on books and trips abroad to the socialist leisure centres on the Black Sea or Hungary's Lake Balaton.

12

A life as a professor's wife with long hair and loose dresses, one who kept quiet when appropriate and took care of the family business. In this life as a spouse I appeared at receptions and celebrations and played the lady in black wearing a lot of chiffon and Indian silk. Apart from this life another soon formed. It belonged to Claude, my lover. He had these green, these sad eyes that I could never get enough of. He could recite poem after poem. I first heard Neruda's "Farewell" from him:* "From deep within you and kneeling / a boy, sad like me, watches us. / For his life to burn in your veins / we would have to bind our lives together ... / For his eyes to open on the world / I will see tears in your eyes someday. / I don't want him, Beloved ..." His love was the counterpoint I needed so that I could endure my public happiness. For behind all the daytime obligations into which I had divided my life at the time stood this incurable hopelessness; I couldn't find words for it and I had gradually trained myself to stop despairing over it. Claude saw through my games of despair even on the first day when we met each other at a party. "Mourning is a parting that never ends," he said to me before he left.

That our love had no future other than the moment in which it happened was the root of our passion, which erupted again and again. That each night of our love could be the last accounted for its ecstasy. Forlornness was the soil in which our love grew, and we were thoroughly in agreement about this condition. We were displaced persons. We knew that the life that had once existed elsewhere could never again be. There could thus be no going back but also no going forward. Forward and back was the moment in which we loved each other.

Claude had emigrated to the GDR following Allende's overthrow. He was bourgeois and belonged to the Chilean Communist Party. This party had strict moral principles for its members in exile. Adultery was forbidden and punishable with expulsion from the GDR. To what extent these principles were arranged with the SED, I do not know.

In any event, our love had to be kept secret twice over: on the one hand, from our spouses, whom we did not want to hurt, and, on the other hand, from the various secret service agencies. A good friend, herself Chilean and wife of a former minister under Allende, helped when she could. Together with her we covered our tracks over and over again and laid down false trails. We promised the secret service a full house where they found an empty one. We invented logistical games.

I was in the thick of it, even though I seemed to be quite distant from the GDR. I learned that even intimate spheres were subject to political control and self-censorship. Even here multiple layers of concealment had become a necessary part of normality for me in order to secure for myself the illusion of a private sphere, for which self-control was the indispensable prerequisite. I do not believe that Claude and I were successful in hiding our love from the various secret services. But my privileged file, like other privileged files from the card index boxes for "prominent persons and their family members," was destroyed by the Stasi shortly after the Wall fell. I was initially furious about this. Today I regard the fact that I cannot know who informed on me as one of my last privileges from the GDR era.

Here among the Chileans I encountered Esther again. She had fallen in love with a writer from Valparaíso and wanted to go with him to Latin America. She wanted to bring the revolution and herself there. By now she sensed that something had gone awry in the GDR. Redemption was not going to happen here. She could not admit it to herself quite so directly, though, so she expressed her desire for a better time by continuing to sing songs of world revolution from the communist choir book. She wanted to get away, as so many did at the time. In the end, "world revolution" was a reason to leave the country, and for Esther it had the additional benefit of not provoking a break with her parents.

Although our reasons for loving the Chileans were contradictory, we were still happy to have found each other again. She baked empanadas on behalf of the "world revolution." I baked empanadas because I wanted nothing to do with it. Together we discovered García Marquez, Jorge L. Borges, Pablo Neruda. I was thrilled by the Mexican painters

Siqueiros and Orózco.* I lived in the songs of Violeta Parra, Victor Jara, and Inti-Illimani.* I lived a life with Claude beyond the GDR – and was still stuck in the middle of the web. For the security forces did not forget about the Chileans in the GDR. Their surveillance was almost overt. So Claude impressed upon me that under no circumstances was I to speak about him with Esther. Her writer was also in the Communist Party. They were *compañeros* and thus, especially for that reason, one had to be cautious. What did he know about this writer, Claude asked, other than that he was a "comrade" and had worked for Luis Covalán, the general secretary of the Chilean Communist Party? Furthermore, Claude insisted, one had to consider the possibility of a connection to "Dina," the Chilean secret service.

As I learned, such considerations regarding the secret services were not only a part of daily interactions in the GDR but also a part of being in love there. For each and every relationship, I had to consider at some point whether "he" or "she" worked for an intelligence service. I hoped that the people I loved were not involved with one in any way. But I was certain only about a very few people in my closest circle, to which Emanuel and Esther belonged. I had learned that children of former spies were only rarely recruited as spies themselves, to guard against conflicts of interest and the possibility of espionage becoming a family business. Since both Esther's and Emanuel's parents had worked for the Soviet intelligence service during the Second World War, I convinced myself that Esther and Emanuel could not be spies. Without the practical certainty that Emanuel and Esther at least did not work for the Stasi, I would have gone crazy. I simply had to believe it.

The prevailing mood of paranoia in the GDR, as I learned at the end of the 1970s, was not country specific, but was part of communist ideology. The enemy was the absolute menace, the incalculable. Since Leninist ideology ruled out the unpredictable – indeed this was a sign of its theoretical superiority – what could not be predicted simply could not be. If something unforeseen nonetheless occurred, it was the work of the enemy, who had to be driven out like the popular medieval figure of the Devil.

So we sat together and sang the Chilean émigrés' songs of better times. Now and then the idea arose that our neighbour might work for this or that secret service. The longer I lived in the GDR, the more living with and among informants became my normal daily routine.

Today it is hard for me to comprehend how former East Germans could feel secure in a country where, as a matter of course, people suspected that a neighbour might be an informant and might even be assigned to spy on them in particular. Perhaps my incomprehension has to do with the fact that I never felt at home in the GDR.

When Emanuel and I moved to Central Berlin (Berlin-Mitte), a family with a child had shortly beforehand rented the neighbouring apartment. Officially, the husband worked for the criminal police. When we moved in he greeted us warmly and helped us from that moment forward. In a touching fashion, he took care of things around the house for us. He repaired faucets, locks, doors, and whatever else needed repair in a socialist apartment in an old building. We knew that he spied on us. If our telephone stopped working, and it always stopped working when Emanuel was travelling in the West, I asked him if he could not get the telephone working again. I told him that if the telephone did not work, there would be nothing to listen in on. Then, alas, I would have to go to a pay phone. Most of the time, the telephone was up and working again within two hours. I thanked my comrade for his speedy assistance. I had a cynical, trusting relationship with my neighbour and appreciated the reliability and correctness with which he did what he did. But with the same correctness with which he looked after our domestic well-being, I always knew that he would also have arrested us if he received the order. He could have offered very properly to look after the apartment and water the flowers when we were away. He knew that I knew it. We were safe in the apartment from burglars. I could even have left the door open. We gave our nice neighbour the key to the front door, so that he could properly attend to things in our absence.

Now and then I had a devilish need to organize pleasant get-togethers even in the presence of every sort of informer. I wanted to test whether my hideout really was secure. So, once or twice a year, I planned parties for no less than fifty guests, that was my scheme. The guests came from the East and the West. The more guests present, the more secure I felt, for the anonymity made personal conversation impossible. At these parties I sought to ascertain whether I had truly succeeded in hiding my face, not only from the various security services, but at all. Amidst the hustle and bustle at such parties I measured the distances, one after the other, in order to determine whether I also wanted to keep my distance. No one should figure out where I actually stood. In addition, I provoked a rendezvous with the secret service with my invitations, since I extended invitations to a lot of foreigners. Over the years I had trained my sense of perfect pitch to the vibrations given off by secret service agents. The acoustics were different when one or two or three different agents were in a room and unloaded their questions and unintentional subordinate clauses and played innocent, when they feigned interest and noted, in the process, who spoke with whom about what. If they observed that I was observing them, then I was not playing my game very well. Nevertheless, during these paranoid games I was convinced that the Stasi wouldn't do anything to me so long as I held to our arrangement and refrained from expressing publicly any sort of political opinion.

Emanuel loved my parties. I never told him why I had them. He found it logical that we were spied on. From time to time, he remarked, all important people were monitored. It was not especially pleasant but it had to be that way, in part for one's own safety: that was Emanuel's belief.

That the Stasi in the post-Stalinist era contributed significantly to that era's decline is, in my opinion, something insufficiently recognizable by looking only at the Stasi's own files. After all, it was principally the Stasi that thwarted any sort of public life and drove East Germany's citizens into the private sphere. Through threats, intimidation, and, as necessary, massive violence, the Stasi prevented the people from expressing themselves in public. As a result, there arose a sort of private public sphere or niche outside the official and publicized existence, which required considerable resources to keep under surveillance, especially in terms of the number of informants that had to be recruited, since such niches could spring up in every home. During the final phase of the disappearance of the state's real political power, the more niches that developed, the more "unofficial collaborators"* were needed for surveillance. And, for the sake of efficiency too, the more the Stasi went about setting up its own niches and taking pains not to let them be discovered.

Ironically, the Stasi can be considered as the former GDR's real "Institute for Opinion Research." It had to find out what people actually thought in order to prevent thinking and action that deviated from official ideology. To that end, every method of brutality was permitted, as long as it served the "cause."

I was right in the middle, although I fancied myself to be outside. So I accustomed myself to the security officers and not just to the one in front of the house of my Chilean friend in Berlin-Niederschönhausen, whose husband was the chairman of the Chilean Socialist Party in exile. Occasionally I even greeted the security officers. I also got used to the security men in front of and inside the governmental hospital that my mother-in-law had to visit more and more. I got used to the guards in front of the government restaurants, where increasingly the family ate, since from year to year it became harder for my mother-in-law to entertain guests at home. During these meals, I obeyed the family rule about not divulging any sort of confidential information to other guests and distinguished persons. Ultimately, one could not be careful enough: there was a risk with any piece of information. This fetishization of information was a rule that had been carried over as a family tradition from the period of illegal activity into daily political life in the GDR and which could also be followed here with some success. For, as paradoxical as it may sound, each of these very important fighters for the common good had a highly unique relationship to the power structure. Their respective personal ties to the members of the political bureaucracy were exceptional and, thus, incomparable. Consequently each distinguished fighter could well feel that he alone had a true and genuine relationship to the Politburo or one of its secretaries, or occasionally even the general secretary.* On top of that, the security services had spun such a complicated web around all the outstanding people that one could never make out – and I least of all – who then had to carry out whose orders for the greater good and, hence, for the greater good, also had to mislead his competitors in order not endanger his personal assignment.

My problem remained that I did not understand what information was confidential and what was not, since the opinions on what counted as confidential, strictly confidential, and public knowledge occasionally changed from one hour to another. Thus, I mainly kept amicably quiet during such meals.

But my problem, too, was that I never understood what actually comprised illegal activity. This was likely related to the fact that I could never seriously believe in The Enemy, and without an enemy illegal activity made no sense. I thus followed the rules of the conspiracy that prevailed within the family: for instance, not to mention any names over the telephone or make any sort of snide political comment about this or that idiotic Party action. I also held fast to the practice of not leaving any addresses lying around in the apartment, out of principle, as Emanuel said, although in this matter my principles were more oriented towards the family peace.

Looking back, I believe that the nomenklatura had the right sense, or, to put it in their terms, the right class instinct, in treating people outside their social position with mistrust and regarding them as potential enemies. Ultimately, every level within the nomenklatura had something to lose. The nomenklatura, in its entirety, was in charge of the People's assets, which it appropriated for itself to the degree it could. It determined where, how, and what should be invested, and took for itself from the People's assets what it thought befitted its status as nomenklatura. But it could only do this as long as it stayed in power politically. The struggle for this power united the nomenklatura into a new class: internally, vis-à-vis the people and, externally, vis-à-vis the capitalist world. To use the language of economics: in my opinion, the new ruling bureaucracy, as Milovan Djilas also called the nomenklatura in his world-renowned book *The New Class*,* had not succeeded in becoming a true class. As it soon became clear, the "ruling bureaucracy" was incapable of reproducing property on the basis of socialism's own theories. So while the East German nomenklatura could certainly dispose of the assets that came into its hands, it was no longer capable of preserving them, let alone generating "capital" from them. In East Germany, it was possible for the politbureaucrats to spend the assets left behind by capitalism until the principal was gone. Indeed, shortly before the end of the socialist planned economy, the paving stones for the sidewalks were still being sold rapidly in the name of this planned economy for hard currency. Without the loans from the West German government and its banks, the end of the GDR would have come some years earlier.

The life of the nomenklatura in the GDR had nothing to do with the life of "our people." For this reason, too, the regular reports "on the state of the working classes and the thinking ranks" could be so falsified from the bottom all the way to the top.

Privileges within the ranks of the nomenklatura were tidily organized. They were differentiated according to the functionary elites' respective interest and share in the retention of power, which again distinguished the various levels and professional classes within the nomenklatura from one another. In the struggle against the undiscerning population, however, they joined forces. Thus, whereas the scholarly elite tended to be fed with Western literature and was allowed reading days in the Western section of Berlin's state library (Staatsbibliothek-West), the elite ranks of the People's Police, who were responsible for maintaining state security and order, had access to more sensual pleasures.

The Interior Ministry, for instance, had its own food service, whose "headquarters," as far as I understood it over the years, were located either in Bad Saarow or Gross-Körris.* One of the miracles that Esther could pull off was to order meals from there by telephone. If her parents were away, she occasionally invited me to their house in Berlin-Niederschönhausen and ordered delicious food from this kitchen – from the finest ham and melons to French cheeses and fresh fruit – which otherwise was unattainable in East Germany. Now and then there was also mussel soup that was so excellent that even today I can recall it. To order such delicacies from the Interior Ministry's service complex one needed a secret number that, for security reasons, I was not permitted to know. Hence, even today I have no idea where the kitchen that made such delicious mussel soup was located. So, once in a while, we sat in the guarded development for state VIPs, which of all things was named after Majakowski,* and ate the mussel soup or the ham with melon, or both, which the Ministry's staff delivered. And in fact, these common meals had something conspiratorial about them, for we took care not to mention them to anyone.

13

While I accustomed myself more and more to the comprehensive surveillance and still did not understand what was confidential and what not, Gorbachev provided for new socialist dreams and hopes. At no time did I believe that Gorbachev would bring salvation, not because I was blessed with any special historical vision but rather because I was incapable of believing in any Messiah who would fix everything – not Christ, not the "new man," and not the Soviet man! There appeared red badges bearing Gorbachev's portrait, with and without the birthmark on his forehead, which initially sold for five marks apiece. The very first of these badges were Western imports that came over the border from enemy territory. The group of elderly politicians around Honecker feared Gorbachev's ideas from the very beginning and, as it turned out, rightly so. Nonetheless, the trade in Gorbachev's head on the red background gained momentum.

Gorbachev's book, *Perestroika,* first appeared in German in the Federal Republic. The East German censorship officials faced the dilemma of not being able to ban the book of the Soviet Communist Party's general secretary. But they could delay its appearance and print it only in limited editions, making the book difficult to obtain. So, a female friend of ours smuggled over the internal German border for us a copy of Gorbachev's thoughts "On the second Russian Revolution" among shrimp from Greenland and vanilla ice cream in an insulated freezer bag from the KaDeWe.*

With its beseeching tone, the text reminded me from the very beginning of Robespierre's speeches to the Convention.* He too charmed the people and called on them to take action; only, what was to be done remained unclear. Gorbachev's book appealed directly to the heart:

we should, we must, we ought! It was a moral flourish, beautiful to read and dream about. But socialism didn't appear in my dreams, so I searched for real suggestions for changing the direction of the economy. But I found no economic concept there, just earnest, warm, imploring, and warning words. Gorbachev hadn't found a way forward! He was only urging people to be better. He demanded good will, just as Kant and Rousseau had already done. But that was not a political-economic analysis that allowed specific conclusions and implied specific actions. The book was just one long series of juxtaposed "ought" statements. I gave Gorbachev no chance at all. In my opinion, wanting to tackle the problems of indiscipline and a bad work ethic with a ban on vodka demonstrated how feeble his entire concept was – especially since the lack of alcohol sales would deprive the state of an important source of tax revenue. Naturally I didn't fathom that Gorbachev was initiating the peaceful dissolution of the "seventy-year experiment with socialism." But in my blindness I was at least in good company, likely including Gorbachev himself.

For the time being, Emanuel and Esther were not alone in singing the songs of *perestroika* and wearing the Gorbachev badges. They dreamed of a new beginning. I couldn't come to terms with their dream. Again I felt cast out. Not by them, no, but rather by my incompetence. Why couldn't I believe in a Messiah? Why couldn't I find a songbook for myself that spoke of hope and better times? Only at the beginning of my time in the GDR did I feel more alone and thrown back on myself. I felt that something in my relationship with Emanuel had irretrievably ended. It had something to do with encouragement, which from then on we were no longer able to offer one another. Claude, sensing my despondency, came back to Neruda's "Farewell": "I do not want it, Beloved. / So that nothing ties us together / that nothing unites us." I had nothing to add to it.

One morning I was standing at the window. A summer sky stretched over the city as far as I could see. I was depressed as I hadn't been in a long time. I had, in fact, learned to get through such days. On that morning, though, I wasn't having any luck even getting started. Without any goal I left the apartment and walked the streets. I stopped before a church located nearby. I had heard that its dean was one of the more intelligent ones. I asked for him. By chance, he was there. I spoke with him about God and how one might reach him. At first he didn't know whether the questions I was asking were really serious. He called me by my last name, saying that he had heard I was a philosopher. I asked him to forget my occupation and name for the moment. Exceptionally, this was about me personally. I gulped – it wouldn't have been appropriate to cry in front of him. He tried using philosophical phrases to answer my questions. I interrupted him: I said that I already knew the philosophical phrases and they didn't help me any more, to the contrary. He stopped, went with me over into the church, and played a few bars on the organ from Bach's Toccata in C Major (BWV 564). Then he looked at me kindly and expectantly. I was furious and felt caught unaware. So, I too sat down at the organ and played the fugue from the same toccata, which is what came to me, until its contrapuntal refinement stopped me. I then left the church without saying a word.

In a way, he was right. If God was anywhere, he was also in music, at least for me. But at the time that didn't help me at all.

14

My time in the GDR was coming to an end. I started to leave the country where I had never felt at home anyway. In 1985 I consciously set out to use my privileges, seeking permission to leave the socialist state temporarily at first in order to recuperate and gain a sense of perspective. There were reasons for granting these requests, since, following the publication of my Hegel book, I had been dubbed an author and was, in fact, writing a novel about my childhood in divided Berlin. Finally, since the novel was set in both the West and the East, research in both sides of the city was essential. Moreover, as I noted to the office of the deputy minister for culture (whose love letters I had smuggled out of the governmental restaurant and carried to his sweetheart), I needed a break from the socialist paradise. I initially received a temporary private visa for West Berlin without, however, having to report on my stay and personal encounters in West Berlin to any GDR authority, which had been required in exchange for the visa when I was at the Academy of Sciences. Later I received a business visa, again one without restrictions, and whether leaving or returning I was rarely subjected to border controls any more.

There was something oppressive about travelling to West Berlin, which was my first trip to a capitalist foreign country in nearly twenty-five years. At the Friedrichsstrasse station, the border checkpoint for entering and leaving East Berlin,* I became frightened. How often had I accompanied my grandmother up to the "Palace of Tears," the border crossing's common nickname?* How often had I waved at her until she disappeared in the dirty neon light of the glass palace? How often had I fought back tears at this spot? Now, it disquieted me to pass through the Palace of Tears and step into the free world, since she no longer lived in this city. All at once my head filled with clichés. I was entering into enemy territory, full of gangsters and criminals. I didn't want to admit it to myself. But they were there, these propaganda images about the West, where one's life was not secure. The oppressive atmosphere at the border checkpoint – the light, the narrow passages to the customs and border police – did not fail to have an effect on me.

In retrospect, it is astonishing that I didn't want to leave. That I was suddenly afraid of leaving the mine-secured "antifascist protective wall" behind which, over time, I had arranged things rather comfortably for myself. I thought about the effect of being confined and the fear of venturing out for a long time, in part because it amazed me that this fear came to me precisely at the border to the outside world, a fear that returned to an ever greater degree when the Wall fell. I read later that this fear of freedom after a long confinement was a symptom frequently experienced by prisoners following their release.

On this occasion, Claude met me at the Friedrichsstrasse border crossing. I was grateful to him. I thus took my first steps in enemy territory alongside my beloved. He gave me a white rose as a symbol of my innocence and went directly with me to the Kaufhaus des Westens (KaDeWe). When, after about an hour, I said that I wasn't feeling very well and was getting light-headed, he laughed contentedly. Thank goodness, he said, because he had undertaken this walk through the KaDeWe only to shock me.

Once we reached Steglitz, I felt more secure in West Berlin.* Nothing much had changed there: it was still what it had been twenty-five years before, an exclusive neighbourhood of apartments and villas. From there we went on to the Schlachtensee. My grandmother had died and her house had been sold. It was summer. We swam twice across the lake, and it was still very cold. Strolling around here was as calming as it had been in my youth. An overwhelming desire arose within me to leave everything behind and run away with Claude. But we knew that it wasn't possible.

I never really was one of them, that is, the antifascist children and their families. No matter how much effort I had made to learn the rules, including those of conspiracy. I didn't just lack political maturity, as they put it, sometimes gently but other times rather critically. I also lacked "family legitimacy." Once again, Esther's mother had put her finger on it more than fifteen years earlier when she asked me one evening, almost in confidence: "And you didn't have even an uncle who had been in the resistance?" No, I didn't have any uncle in the resistance. I didn't have any uncles at all. And it didn't occur to me then to invent one.

My parents were simply fellow travellers, German fellow travellers in a war that had profoundly damaged them. But this didn't really qualify as a mitigating factor in the eyes of the antifascist families, who again were mainly of Jewish origin. However much they tried not to notice that I didn't actually belong, the distance remained, partly because it was also cultural. To the extent that this distance reflected their intellectual worldliness, I could overcome it as I came to understand their cultural world. The distance that was founded on their faith in communism, however, was impossible for me to bridge. When this belief in communism came about through a simple change in faith – as with Esther's mother, whose father had been a rabbi – a certain continuity between the old and the new religion could be maintained. For they still belonged to a chosen people, one that had made a covenant with "history" and had pledged to be faithful to its laws.

The majority of East Germany's communist Jews, though, had lost their religious ties to Judaism already two and three generations before. With the scientific variant of assimilation, namely via a confession of faith in communism and its Marxist-Leninist world view, the problem of assimilation seemed in fact to have been solved universally, by seemingly sublimating Judaism into international solidarity and worldwide brotherhood. This identity, which had been constructed over generations, was now shaken as socialism approached its end. Less so by the parents than by the antifascist children, who once more raised questions about their actual identity. It is thus hardly surprising that precisely these children discovered the Jewish community in the 1980s and that they recollected in public that they were Jewish children.

As they sought to find themselves, many of them questioned their parents' apparent certainty that through assimilation they could cancel out their Jewish origins with internationalism and worldwide revolution. In the process, they correctly sensed that the Jewish community could also grant them protection through differentiation. The isolation and eccentricity of many antifascist children could initially be retained here, as could their "natural privileges." Thus the Jewishness of many of these children was discovered in the 1980s as a niche within the society of niches.* Eccentric and alienated as socialism neared its end, their need for differentiation produced some grotesque blossoms. For instance, the first Jewish wedding in the East Berlin community took place in this period. Emanuel was invited and, naturally we went together. At the entrance to the community centre, though, I was stopped and informed that, at the bride's request, only Jews were being admitted to the ceremony. Emanuel laughed out loud. When he realized that this was no joke, he did an about-face and was rather disgusted. He mumbled something about Semites in the Jewish community and didn't set foot in the synagogue again during the GDR era.

There was thus a certain logic to the hero-children's return to their Jewish past. To it also belonged the transition, completed two and three years later, of some antifascist children from the Marxist-Leninist state church to the Jewish community as a shelter from the confusion of the times. After the Chilean writer had left her, thus, it was not by chance that Esther sought to join the Jewish congregation. That Esther, the daughter of the first and only Jewish major general in the GDR's history, then married the East Berlin congregation's only guest rabbi, an American no less, was a political metaphor for her emotional state.

Through the revaluation of things Jewish towards the end of the GDR era, efforts to improve relations with Israel tempted the SED leadership to improve economic relations with the United States. The goal of these efforts was supposedly a state visit for Honecker in Washington. And so much had East Germany's economic experts understood: such a visit would not be possible without the American Jewish community's consent. That it was now in the GDR's interest to view Jewishness positively, something unthinkable previously, in turn allowed the antifascist hero-children to keep their faith alive while still remaining true to East Germany. Thus, after some hesitation, Esther, the singer of better and fairer times, left East Germany in May 1988. She did so as a rabbi and with the Politburo's official blessing so that, upon arriving in the United States, the class enemy, she could seek asylum and a green card. She didn't just change her religion: for in marrying the Polish-born rabbi and Auschwitz survivor she found a way to connect the vestiges of her antifascist childhood to her new life in the United States.

The GDR was finished before it finally collapsed, and not just for me. Its economic experts tried to obtain hard currency wherever they could. And for a while, it seemed to the East German bureaucrats that the Jewish lobby in the United States was ready to do more than just invest in rebuilding the Berlin Synagogue.*

While Esther turned to the Jewish community, I turned to the American Jews who regularly spent some of their summer vacations in Germany as friends of the family, many of whom had also become my own friends. Over the years I had followed their reports on the world and global political events with interest. For years, what they reported about the outside world, together with the Chileans' reports and their views on world events, was enough for me. I took the news from "outside" into my hideout with me and assembled for myself the little piece of the world that was freely delivered to me at home. This would greatly facilitate my political orientation after 1989. That many Jewish intellectuals did not come to a similar point before the Wall fell, because they couldn't fathom why a good bourgeois Jewish intellectual like Jürgen Kuczynski would have allowed himself to be made into a fool by a courtly state of very limited intellectual capabilities, was something I learned only in the years after 1989.

So I turned to the family's friends. I said that I wanted to get out. Not away, but out. I gave up the role of the professor's wife with the long hair and debated in an intellectually mature fashion, spoke about my political views that I had formed in my hideout high in the trees, and spoke too about my observations on life in the gardens of the nomenklatura. Friends took my book on Hegel and job application materials with them to the United States. They said that they would take care of things for me, and they did. Roughly six months later I received an invitation and a fellowship from the Council for European Studies at Columbia University in New York as well as a visiting professorship in the College of Arts and Sciences at the State University of New York, Buffalo.

I took the invitation to the Ministry of Culture. The woman responsible for such matters there muttered that this just would not be possible, she had never had such a case before. So again I requested an appointment with the deputy minister for cultural affairs. I told him that if I weren't granted a visa for the United States, we would have to discuss why the Main Office for Censorship still hadn't approved the publication of the novel that I had finished more than a year ago, *Wenn ich kein Vogel wär* (If I Were Not a Bird).

The deputy minister told me that I should complete a detailed visa application, explaining what I planned to do in the United States, and give it to him in his office. Together with Emanuel I completed the application, along with a lecture and travel itinerary for the United States, and received the visa, directly from the travel department in Honecker's office. That the approval for the trip was turned into an issue for the government reflected more the pettiness of the government's interests, though, than the trip's own importance.

And thus, I discovered that even I could get what I wanted from the powers that be. For me personally, this was the most important thing I learned while preparing for my trip to the United States. It meant that, in all likelihood, I would also be able to get my way in the future.

The trip to the United States wasn't just the end of my compulsory residence in East Germany. It was, at the same time, my beginning in the "brave new world" that then arrived in East Germany two years later, after the GDR's citizens had finally set out, by foot and by train, to see paradise for themselves.

Frank, a friend from West Berlin who had married a New Yorker, waited for me at Kennedy Airport. He took my hand, for the fear was there once again. Fear of "the freedom" of the unknown. Fear of taking my own steps outside the supervised state, which I now had to do in such a vast and dangerous city as New York.

Carefully, I took one step after another and measured the fear in relation to the years in which it had built up. It worried me in those first days. But then, right at 107th Street behind Columbia University, I suddenly went running and raced down Broadway. My fear dissolved and passed into the endlessly wonderful feeling of being free. At 72nd Street I stood still, closed my eyes, and listened to the rhythm of the New York traffic. The speed of the steps with which the pedestrians passed me by stuck in my head, as did the loudness of the stream of cars, which came to a stop only for the traffic lights. I absorbed the sound of the horns that never wanted to stop. Blended into the sound were the sirens of the police cars. They kept the city noises in a balance that I had never heard before.

I was free. I realized that on 72nd Street in Manhattan. Even the question of whether I would go back behind the Wall was something I could decide for myself. For the first time in my life I could choose freely between the two world systems. With this feeling I walked through the city. I was intoxicated by its vastness, excited by its size. I walked for hours. Over and over, I stopped to see myself in relation to the skyline, and then I moved forward in order to get away from it again. I wanted to measure the skyscrapers' heights, and the amount of sky that remained above them. I hid myself in the skyscrapers' shadow, there where hardly any more light fell, crouched, and wrote a poem to them. I took its rhythm from the street. Then I continued on. I was on the way to Rockefeller Center. I wanted to have lunch there with a friend. I stood there, high above Manhattan, and looked out the windows at the city while a scarcely controllable rage arose within me. Those Politburo bureaucrats and tottering old men of the nation – on their account I was never in my life to set eyes on all of this! Not New York, not the Atlantic Ocean, also not the Pacific, not the Mississippi, not the Rocky Mountains, and not San Francisco either. I began to sense that I had missed out on quite a lot living in the security block of the First Workers' and Peasants' State's secured zones, where I had arranged things rather comfortably for myself.

I flew from one end of the United States to the other and enjoyed its vastness. I was downright addicted to it. Along the way, I gave lectures on Hegel and on classic German philosophy. I read from my novel, *Wenn ich kein Vogel wär*. Friends had smuggled the manuscript out of East Germany. I did what I had never managed to do in East Germany: speak freely and without fear. For the first time since I resigned from the Academy of Sciences I talked about philosophy, and I spoke without any self-imposed censorship. Fortunately, I had forgotten it during my years as a housewife. Even the old cleverness, which one needed to dance around the censorship, failed to come back to me. As a result of the years of disguising myself as a housewife, I had become sure of myself again. I could now calmly say that I didn't know something and was glad not to have to know everything anymore. I had become more relaxed and perhaps also more confident. I tried out being both in the United States.

I realized that my specialist knowledge would outlive the GDR. It was more than I had expected. With Hegel and classic German philosophy I hadn't intellectually survived just the GDR. I could also build on my knowledge outside of East Germany. It would endure. I received a live confirmation of this at the American universities. The students didn't just show interest in what I said because they had been well brought up. They also raised the most pertinent questions that were to be asked about classical German philosophy. Through philosophy, thus, I could communicate outside of the GDR. And not only at Columbia University's philosophy department, where many German emigrants and expatriates had assembled after 1933 and into the 1950s. At other universities, too, there were philosophy and German departments with well-trained students and specialists.

Yet, happy as I was that my specialized skills could hold their own, I was still bored with them, even outside of the socialist camp. In East Germany, I was already tired of everything that had to do with Hegel. The problem that I wanted to solve with philosophy's help had been solved. I realized that there couldn't be a solution to it. "Where did I come from?" "Where am I going?" and "Why am I here?" – I realized that these were eternal questions that could never be answered within an existence bounded by space and time.

Now I was addicted to seeing and living. The structures of philosophy, no matter how refined, no longer astonished me. Simplicity amazed me much more now. For instance, at the Museum of Modern Art, I became fascinated by Picasso's wood-hewn "Nanny Goat." I stood in front of it for hours. I couldn't get enough of the clarity of his lines or the point of view that Picasso presented so straightforwardly here.

I enjoyed my time in the United States and flew from one city to another. The Stasi flew either after or ahead of me. In any event, a female Stasi agent – whom I already knew from my time in East Germany – was always where I would next be arriving or departing. I had a cynical relationship with her and gave my regards to her, wherever she happened to turn up. The American "middle class" was touchingly innocent when it came to the intelligence services. My colleagues at the university joyfully told me that my countrywoman had just been there or that she would be arriving just after I had left. And they regretted that we kept flying past one another. I regretted it too, insincerely, and noted that the Stasi wanted to let me know that it was watching me.

For me, there was something surreal about the Stasi in the United States. I could never take them seriously. The FBI, by contrast, had impressed me. At the German Studies Association's conference in St Louis, a good-looking man sat next to me at one of the dinners. He introduced himself as an FBI agent and then told me about all the problems my entry had caused his agency. On my papers for a visa I had written "housewife" in the rubric for "current occupation" – which technically was my status in East Germany. I had registered neither as a freelancer nor as being anyone's employee. But what did the FBI know of such GDR games? Apparently nothing. For the FBI, my case was one they had never had before: a German housewife who travels to Columbia University as a Hegel specialist, related the good-looking man, laughing. They thought that this was perhaps a brand-new generation of GDR agents. He raised his glass and wished me a continued good stay in the United States. After this conversation I remembered that my visa for entering the United States had arrived only the day before I departed. Friends had interceded on my behalf at the State Department.

My stay in the United States was at once a beginning and an end: it was thus important to me that I experienced the "modern world" in its purest form. Not in its pampered Western European version, but rather in the full force of its capitalist contradictions, so that in its extremes I felt free and independent for the first time. I could no longer take seriously my previous "day trips in West Berlin" as voyages into another land, and by no means could I regard them as arrivals in another world system.

I observed the force of contradictions as never before in the United States: the division of society into rich and poor without a social safety net; the slums in the big cities; the violence, which was latent everywhere. When shooting broke out two metres from me in New York, a female friend grabbed my arm and said: Let's go, you can't do anything anyway. She was in fact entirely correct, but what deeply impressed me was how natural it all seemed to her. I was also struck by the naturalness with which the extremes suddenly changed as soon as we arrived on the university campus, finding ourselves all at once in a beautiful, safe world. For everything here possessed a graciousness and an intellectual charm that even today evokes in me the wish to live in one of those countless, idyllic university towns.

Two years later, following East Germany's entry into the Federal Republic of Germany, this force of contradictions helped me considerably to put my travails in the unified German welfare state into perspective.

There were many reasons for my return to East Germany after being in the United States, but no political reason. Or at most, the awareness that I would be able to leave again. That I didn't remain in the United States had much to do with Emanuel and the family, but it also had become clear to me how difficult it would be to live in the United States as a writer, on the one hand because of my native language and, on the other, because of my finances. For I sensed that nowhere else were intellectuals and artists who were critical and true to the state taken as seriously as in the socialist countries. Nonetheless I still had taken copies of my graduate certificate and doctoral diploma with me. And a friend had already brought a copy of my dissertation from Berlin to the States. I left everything there and went back.

At the Friedrichsstrasse border crossing I was asked for my "count card" (*Zahlkarte*). I didn't understand. After I figured it out, I realized that they were asking about a pink card that was buried deep in my suitcase. These were handed out by customs officials for statistical and security purposes whenever one left or entered East Germany and had to be filled out and surrendered upon entry. I said that I didn't have the card anymore and they made clear to me that I couldn't re-enter the country without it. I exploded with laughter. An officer came and tried to clear up the matter. I quickly made up a story, since I had no desire at all to unpack my suitcase in the middle of the Friedrichsstrasse station. The story was simple: I was robbed at my hotel in Miami. Not only did my money disappear, but also my transfer card. Thankfully, I had deposited my passport in the hotel safe. The officer took it all down. He finished his report and asked if I could still remember the day this occurred. I made one up, signed the report, and knew that I had returned to the First Workers' and Peasants' State.

The East German authorities never once asked about my trip to the United States. Apparently, as a member of the nomenklatura in a socialist dictatorship, I now had just as much freedom as a fool in a medieval court to do what I pleased.

15

Socialism gave out without anyone suspecting that it was coming to an end, and not just in the GDR. To many people, the socialist end seemed to be a renewed beginning, and Gorbachev its leader. In the subtitle to his book, *Perestroika,* he had called for a "second Russian Revolution," admitting thereby that, for better or worse, the first had gone awry.

And for a moment it looked as if this ending, too, was also a beginning, since, in East Germany at least, the beginning of socialism's demise lay so far back in the past. Indeed, had the Soviet tanks not stopped the people's uprising of 17 June 1953, the socialist experiment in Germany would have ended thirty-five years earlier.

Who would be surprised that, again, it was mainly East German intellectuals who became the dreamers of a "second Russian Revolution"? They lived so disconnected from "the people" and from the facts that they couldn't appreciate that "our people" had had enough of socialist asceticism long ago. They were already in the process of exchanging the promises of a better and brighter future for headlights that could actually light up the highway in front of their fifteen-year-old cars. They were on their way, too, to a replacement for the socialist promises that had never been kept.

In the GDR as well, utopias remained first and last the stuff of intellectuals' dreams. "Our people" had abandoned those dreams long ago and were now busy reformulating their requests. For that, they would need to make telephone calls so that, among other things, they knew where they could find tiles for the bathroom or cement. Most people, however, didn't have a telephone, and the waiting period for a connection still stood at ten years.

After the street demonstrations had occurred and the socialist experiment peacefully came to an end, the intellectuals resented that the people had other dreams. Most of the intellectuals were disappointed, not with their grandiose misjudgments of the historical facts and what the people wanted, but rather with the "East German citizenry." The majority of socialist intellectuals found it distasteful that East Germans desired bananas, shower gel, and cars and not the complete works of Nietzsche or Trotsky.

The end remained the end. They had not reached the "promised land" via a socialist path. And like all the great religions, socialism had now reached that stage where the founders were confronted by the fact that their ideas about how to achieve salvation from all worldly evil had themselves become the evil of fixed dogma.

The beginning in the end – for a moment that's again how it appeared. It was hardly surprising that precisely those hero-children who were still in the country wanted to hang on to it; after all, they owed their sense of their life's purpose to this socialist utopia.

But no matter how uncertain and ambivalent I remained about my life's purpose, I never considered it to involve creating a socialist communal utopia on earth. So I didn't see the need to contribute to the world revolution by continuing the socialist experiment. I took part neither in the reformers' campaign nor that of the East German opposition. The former group, working with Gorbachev, wanted to reform socialism in order to keep it. They proudly called themselves socialist reformers. The others, socialist dissidents from Biermann to Bahro,* and the opposition figures from the 1980s, wanted to keep socialism so that they could change it, which basically amounted to the same thing. In contrast to the reformers, who had well-paid, life-long positions in the state institutes for the social sciences and who swam with the current of the times, the dissidents had risked jail and shown a certain degree of civil courage, which set them apart morally from the reformers. The rival brothers both wanted a socialist society, they just wanted one that was truer and purer than what in fact existed. For the most part, East German dissidents remained Marxists and criticized revolutionary theory with their own theoretical resources. Consequently, they remained prisoners of Marxism, and at times Leninism too. They wanted to make the theory conform to the historical givens so as not to put off any longer the construction of their imaginary future. They wanted socialism.

When I returned from the United States, I knew even better than before that the greater good of humanity was not my cause, and could relate even less to the quarrelling faith communities. Over the years I had made an effort to fit in, but I no longer did so now. I hadn't succeeded in sacrificing myself for the greater good. I had retained some small bit of my own integrity, and I was at last happy about that. I had trained myself over the years to disregard the socialist guilt complex that marked my behaviour as morally egoistic. When I still did become emotionally agitated, it was a diffuse, residual anger towards the socialist bureaucracy's demands and towards the inane propaganda that I encountered in my daily life. In therapy I had learned not to direct my powerless rage at the socialist conditions against myself in the form of aggression. I had learned to neutralize the aggression. For twenty-three hours of the day, I didn't care about socialism. During the twenty-fourth hour, I tried to control myself so I didn't explode. I could turn off socialism too. That was another result of the psychoanalysis, which the socialist orthodoxy was justified in banning, since it enabled individuals to remove themselves from everyday life under socialism and contemplate things for themselves.

Nevertheless, my powerlessness vis-à-vis what I had experienced during more than twenty-eight years of living in the GDR proved to have long-term effects. The trauma of the Wall, which I had never been able to cope with, had psychologically marked me. The powerlessness I had experienced had broken my faith in one's ability to shape history. I had no chance against the superior strength of the socialist state that confronted me in the form of the Wall. This experience was the root of the historical fatalism that had settled in me over time. The more I internalized it, the more "ripe" I became, against my will, for the socialist life. It no longer occurred to me to act socially as an individual. I had "recognized," had "understood," that nothing could be done and that "history" prevailed over everything. I had rationalized my personal powerlessness with respect to the circumstances. And who, if not Hegel, provided first-class arguments for it? I found the basis for my fatalistic position in his *Philosophy of History*: Progress in the consciousness of freedom already takes its world historical course. History is the progress of the rational. The world spirit (*Weltgeist*) will not allow itself to be led astray by a spiritless present. This spiritless present, which is an alienated stage of this world spirit, cannot hold up the course of world history for very long. This was my political credo for all these years. One article of which was that, regardless of me, world history will judge the activities of the world spirit.

With such an arrogant but convenient position I had fully accommodated myself to the repressive society. With this position I could calmly run around in the gardens of the nomenklatura. So when I came into contact with the activists, I felt sorry for them for believing that people could somehow affect history through their own actions.

During this time, the distance between Emanuel and myself grew, and it grew from both sides. Emanuel worked tirelessly on behalf of *perestroika*. He knew that if the experiment went awry, he and his life would hang along with it. And I knew that if I didn't join in, I would lose him. The silence between us grew. We settled into it and, after more than fifteen years of marriage, had enough of a routine that we didn't get on each other's nerves or get in each other's way. In short, we tolerated each other's work, but no longer took interest in it. Hugs and embraces, which we previously had been able to rely on in order to overcome our extreme positions, no longer helped. Every conversation increased the distance between us; it breached the fundamental agreement underlying our relationship, which was not to talk about political differences.

My loneliness in the GDR increased. To get through it, I hit on the idea to move. The apartment Wieland Herzfelde had from the Academy of the Arts was available. Wieland Herzfelde was a literary scholar who had founded the Malik publishing house in the 1920s. A Jewish intellectual, he had emigrated after 1933 and then came to East Germany after 1945. His brother, the graphic artist John Heartfield, was a co-founder of the Dada art movement's Berlin branch. And now Wieland Herzfelde had decided to move into a retirement home for antifascist resistance fighters.

In a larger apartment, the distances between Emanuel and myself would perhaps be bearable. Besides, the apartment was in a wonderful location and also nearby to my in-laws. The idea that we would be living just around the corner appealed strongly to my mother-in-law, who always needed help in her big house. In addition, living so close by, we'd be able to put up the family's guests. Hence, my mother-in-law herself promoted the idea that Emanuel and I trade our four-room place for the two-hundred-square-metre, six-room apartment, which of course made a mockery of the notion of equality in living conditions in the GDR. But prominent East Germans didn't just have special pools of cars, telephones, and video recorders, they also had a separate stock of apartments. I remember that there had been a fair amount of fighting over the Academy of Arts' apartment and that other prominent members of the elite were furious that we, of all people, received the apartment and not they, which ultimately the SED district office and not the housing authority awarded to us.

Yes, the privileges: although I possessed them as a "member" and now exploited them cynically, East German citizens who were neither VIPs nor belonged to the nomenklatura strove all the more adamantly for them. While I recovered from my trip to the West in the GDR's stale air, citizens drafted petitions to the Council of State to be allowed to travel. Those who lost patience applied for exit visas or formed opposition groups under the Church's protection. While I consciously settled down in the GDR and, even more symbolically, moved into a "stately" apartment, in Berlin-Marzahn the keys of the three millionth new apartment building (according to real socialism's falsified statistics; more accurate calculations suggest it was only the two millionth) were handed to Erich Honecker. These new socialist apartments were commonly called "workers' lockers" because they were so small. While I organized with my construction crew the theft of insulated windows for the kitchen and baths from the state-owned construction conglomerate and illegally paid them large sums of money to renovate my apartment during their normal working hours, Emanuel worked tirelessly for *glasnost*. It was of little interest to him where the sinks and the floor tile for the bathroom came from. To be safe, I told him nothing about my having paid for this stealing. While I had new wood floors put in and sealed with varnish from the Intershop,* the Soviet newspaper *Sputnik* was stricken from the list of printed materials that could be received by mail in the GDR, because it reported too much on *glasnost* in the Soviet Union. Emanuel was so outraged that he backed the writing of a protest letter in his Institute. That gave rise to heated arguments, and not just within the Academy administration. Emanuel subjected himself to mild self-criticism, so as not to endanger his Institute, and stomached his humiliation "for the cause."

In Leipzig, the "Initiative for a Democratic Renewal of Our Society" called out for a demonstration. I was so disconnected from the GDR that I was never once curious to hear what the "renewal of our society" was supposed to mean. For me East Germany had become a place to which, in the future, I wanted to return after my trips to the West in order to write in peace.

To the extent that the estrangement between Emanuel and me grew, my need for financial independence also increased. Since my novel, *Wenn ich kein Vogel wär*, was never approved for publication, I decided to submit an outline for a film based on the book to the state-owned German Film Corporation (Deutsche Film Aktiengesellschaft or DEFA), without saying that a book on the subject already existed. The outline was accepted. That wasn't all that unusual. DEFA squandered vast amounts of money for "script developments" that never became films. The outline was followed by a treatment and then a scenario. Suddenly I was earning so much money that I had to give up my status as housewife and declare myself a freelance artist, for my supplemental income now exceeded many times over what housewives were allowed to earn. My freelance status led to an offer from DEFA to conduct research in West Berlin for the film. In the summer of 1988, I received a visa that allowed me to leave and enter the GDR at will – without ever having to push for it. It was the customary offer made to artists, designed to encourage their loyalty to the GDR, since the visa could be revoked again for misbehaviour. Among other things, this visa meant that I would no longer be subject to inspections on the East German side of the border. And now that I had a "business visa," I wouldn't be asked anymore about my visits in West Berlin or West Germany, neither by the Stasi nor by anyone else. But when I picked up the business visa at the Ministry of Culture, the deputy minister of culture suggested that I register with the writers' union so that my visa had an official sponsoring authority. I was told that since I was now working as a freelancer, the Office of the Ministry of Culture was no longer responsible for me. So I signed up with the writers' union, remarking that the deputy minister of culture wished me to register there. They were courteous to me, with an obsequiousness that I utterly despised – and not just in cultural bureaucrats. Only after the Wall fell, in December 1989, though, did I officially become a member of the East German writers' union.

Yes, the privileges: the history of East Germany's downfall could be described as the story of how these were democratically watered down, for it was also a struggle for an equal right to privileges. In other words, to the same extent that the GDR was brought to its knees politically and economically, the ruling politbureaucracy tried to exert control over a broader distribution of privilege, which, in the long run, could no longer be controlled. Through the ever more differentiated granting of special rights, that is, special freedoms, it sought to isolate the individual professional classes and social ranks from one another in order to play them off one another and enforce discipline. Discipline, since this granting of privileges was sanctioned by neither document nor seal, but depended rather on the individual's good conduct and obedience.

The higher and, thus, more important a professional class was ranked for preserving the state's political power, the greater the proportion of princely caprice and favour that came into play. So, for instance, almost all the "important artists and other socialist personalities" also had their own personal contact person in either the SED Central Committee or the Politburo. They could present their special requests and complaints there and naturally also their general concerns regarding "our socialist Republic." Whether and how these wishes would be granted depended on the mood of the relevant Central Committee secretary or Politburo member, his personal feelings towards the specific artist as well, but also the party functionary's educational level. The whole privilege business was almost entirely extralegal, thus capricious. That is, except for the privileges of the "antifascist resistance fighters," there was hardly any legal basis for any of this apart from the special pensions established for individual professional classes.

In contrast to the privileges under feudalism, to which socialism was often compared, the entire business of privileges under socialism was never formalized through written documents or public seals, as was customary under medieval constitutions. Socialist privileges were not negotiated among "estates, ranks, and monarchs" but were rather given by "God's grace" and "royal will" and could be revoked at any time. They were instruments of political domination and not just a retreat from bourgeois-democratic fundamental rights.

The closer socialism came to an end, the clearer it became that, under socialism, privileges were just the result of horse trading between the powers that be and the professional classes or individual people. The more the GDR fell apart, the more its citizens demanded the same privileges for everyone, for the state could now be blackmailed. The more preoccupied the politbureaucracy was with granting an individual's special needs, the less it could fulfil the general public's social demands. The East German Council of State made decisions about the distribution of water faucets and about Citizen Helga B's trip to her aunt in Bavaria, instead of looking after the desolate economy. East German citizens composed petition after petition on publicly owned typewriters during working hours in order to obtain what others already had: a telephone, a car, a trip. No matter how separately these people lived in their niches, the socially differentiated professional classes and political groups, they were united in demanding – albeit independently of one another – what they didn't yet have: their special freedoms in the form of privileges. Separate, everyone for oneself, they exacted concession after concession and were, consequently, busy and on the move for the same cause, namely, to set aside the business in privileges as an instrument of the politbureaucracy's power. When at last everyone had the same privileges, the ability to travel in particular, the GDR collapsed. The democratic watering down of privilege thus became the pivotal issue in the articulation of democratic-civic demands. The struggle for the same rights for everyone and thus the same freedoms for everyone – to travel, to speak, to write, and to believe – brought the GDR closer step by step to political ruin. For the most part, thus, the citizens' movement fought contrary to its self-understanding not so much for a democratic renewal of socialism on German soil as for the *de facto* establishment of fundamental civil-democratic rights, which were incompatible and could never be reconciled with the dictatorship of the proletariat. The citizens' movement in East Germany fought for bringing about these rights, which had been pushed through in the Federal Republic of Germany after the Second World War with the help of the occupying powers. Hence, it could in fact be said that the peaceful revolution in East Germany had terminated the bourgeois Revolution of 1848 on German soil. At the same time, by signing the Helsinki Accords in 1975* the East German government had created the legal grounds for the civil rights movement and also, against all expectations, the legal grounds for its own political demise.

While the citizens' movement organized the peaceful revolution, I was busy with the upgrades to our apartment. While I coordinated the craftsmen's activities and kept up everyone's spirits with my homemade lunches every day, Emanuel was busy day and night renovating the socialist house, with *perestroika*. He took only limited interest in my extensive construction project. I had only limited interest in his renovations of socialism. Since I didn't bother him further with my construction project nor he me with his socialist renovations, we peacefully moved into the new apartment in July 1989. We had both been rather exhausted by our respective projects, my construction work and his renovations, and so I succeeded in persuading Emanuel to stop his work on political renewal and *glasnost* for two or three weeks to go on vacation. That would give us a chance to appreciate having mastered the move of our 250 numbered boxes of books, especially after the movers had piled about half of the book boxes in the middle of the large, forty-square-metre hallway up to the ceiling without any damage to the structure of the house, which had been built in 1912.

It was a grand house and we were welcomed to it with flowers. Artists, doctors, and professors were its tenants. Since the housing association had never properly maintained it, there were constantly power outages and problems with the water. One night, when another such malfunction became apparent, the other tenants woke us. Still in our bathrobes, our socialist household searched for the source of the problem from the cellar to the attic and, though half asleep, remembered to tell Frau Doktor and Herr Professor to be careful not to fall over their own slippers in the dark hallway.

Despite the ever-growing alienation, our routine as a married couple allowed us to maintain friendly relations between ourselves. So in September 1989 we travelled to one of the Academy's hostels for the leadership elite. In the end, Emanuel loved the idea of not being in Berlin for the fortieth anniversary of the GDR's founding.* As an enthusiastic Gorbachev sympathizer, he found himself coming increasingly into conflict with the East German flavour of socialist politics and was content with the idea of not having to attend the jubilee celebrating the GDR's fortieth birthday.

Thus, while more than fifty thousand East Germans were making their way to West Germany via Budapest following the opening of Hungary's border with Austria,* we were on our way into rural Brandenburg to recover from *perestroika*, social reorganization, and my construction project. At the same time that the citizens' movement founded groups like "Democracy Now" and "Democratic Renewal," in the Märkischen Schweiz* I began work on a new novel. I had even asked for a typewriter to be brought from my study in Berlin.

In my desire to ignore the oppositional and citizens' movements, I was at least in good company – as I later discovered. For the GDR wasn't alone in not wanting any changes in Germany. The Federal Republic also had no interest at all in real political change, much less reunification. In both German states the establishment was quite comfortable with the status quo, and they were proud of the peaceful relations they had cultivated with one another. The buffets, and not just at academic receptions, were also literally more tasteful and attested to the GDR's greater worldliness. The Social Democrats in West Germany (SPD) were at the height of their politics of détente and were savouring their diplomatic successes, which included being on good terms with the first German Workers' and Peasants' State. But neither did the opposition forces want to spoil this achievement. The Christian

Democrats (CDU) rolled out the red carpet for Honecker.* In both East and West Germany things were going well for the political establishment. It enjoyed the fruits of its many years of efforts to hold talks in a relaxed atmosphere and it was not about to let the opposition groups and the democracy movement talk it to death now. Both sides benefited from an advance on their savings, even if it was drawn on different accounts. East Germany overdrew its cash accounts, West Germany its political accounts. It was for this reason that the West German government strove to prevent the worst-case scenario, namely East Germany's collapse.

While seventy thousand people demonstrated in Leipzig, I gathered mushrooms and strung them on some yarn to dry. While the elderly political leaders delighted in a laser show in front of the Palace of the Republic on the evening of 7 October 1989 and Handel's Royal Fireworks Music resounded from the colour television in the Academy's hostel, I was busy planning the menu for lunch the next day. I had planned chanterelles and beef steak, but we never ate them, since Emanuel had called Berlin yet again and decided that he must return. Grumbling about it would have been pointless. Wordlessly I packed up our things. The next morning we drove to the revolution, which was already in full swing.

After twenty-eight years in East Germany, I had become so immunized to political movements that I largely succeeded in tuning out current events in their entirety. I had become so apathetic towards political action that I initially hadn't sensed that more had been set in motion here politically than had ever occurred previously in East Germany. I succeeded in writing myself into my new novel. And, in a fanciful way, it was related to the GDR's downfall. For Esther's departure from the real socialist GDR had affected me more than I at first wanted to admit. I was both sad and angry that the singer of the revolution had left. Her "Song of a Small Trumpeter" and "It Burns, Brothers, It Burns" now seemed orphaned. Her songs came to me unexpectedly when she called from America to hear about what was going on here and how I was doing. What is more, I had even persuaded her to leave. But she would not have been allowed to leave, not her. That was the stuff for a novel. "The Children of the Red Aristocracy" was its working title.

I took my first step towards the political door on 4 November by going to the demonstration that had been organized by artists and the "New Forum." More than ten years had passed since I had attended a demonstration. Not that I grasped what was going on historically, but I at least noticed that this demonstration was refreshingly different from those that I could remember.

With the Wall's collapse on 9 November I finally woke up from my deep political slumber. On that very day a female friend from West Berlin was visiting me. Around 11:00 p.m., I took her to the S-Bahn headed towards the Friedrichsstrasse checkpoint, so that she left "New Germany" (that is, the GDR) before midnight, as was required. More out of habit than curiosity, I turned on the television to hear what ARD or ZDF had for late evening news.* All the channels were carrying the same footage. I called my friend in West Berlin. She hadn't noticed anything at the Friedrichsstrasse checkpoint, only that the U-Bahn was fuller than usual. Her sixteen-year-old son, however, had told her that something was going on and had just taken off with his graffiti spray paint. He wanted to be a professional sprayer and never missed opportunities to leave his views about the political state of the world on the walls.

I sat spellbound in front of the television. At some point Emanuel joined me. Neither one of us was especially happy with the news, although for very different reasons. Emanuel repeated several times the line: "Such political nonsense to open up the Wall. You couldn't dream it up!" I don't know how long I had been sitting in front of the television before I finally turned off the test pattern on ARD. At some point, I began to weep bitterly. With rare clarity I knew that the GDR's days were now numbered, since without the Wall the East German state would have gone bust twenty-eight years ago. I understood, too, that my life in the gardens of the nomenklatura was over. An indescribable rage came over me, for I was at last trying to make a place for myself in the GDR. I had just stopped quarrelling with God and the world. After twenty-eight years of East Germany, I had finally come to terms with the madness by writing and wanted to do everything I could to keep my identity. The thought that the Wall would again have a hand in my fate infuriated me profoundly. I wouldn't have the energy to begin my life over for a third time. After all, it had taken me some twenty years to cut out those pieces of me that couldn't survive in this country and put them in the deep freeze. At first in slices, and then in small portions, I had packaged up piece after piece of myself and placed them in the freezer. I wouldn't find the strength to defrost the deep-frozen package and make it part of me again. The frostbite was irreversible. The death that I had died, before I had settled into a life behind the Wall, was genuine. I had killed off too much within me. For I had insisted that only I would lay a hand on myself. I had sworn that to myself on the blue oxygen tanks that stood next to my bed after I woke up for a third time in the intensive care unit and a doctor asked me the idiotic question of whether I wasn't ashamed of trying to kill myself. I had no right to do such a thing, he meant, given the amount of real suffering in the world. Only after this vow did I stand up and begin to play the part of a reasonable person. The self-protection that existed in an overdose of phenobarbital, whose expiration date I carefully monitored, was part of this reasonability game. The more reasonable I became, the easier it was to obtain the poison. But it was also part of this reasonability game that for twenty-eight years in East Germany I dragged around the lug wrench that I had stolen while under psychiatric treatment at the beginning of my time behind the Wall, for I never again wanted to end up involuntarily in a psychiatric clinic. The wrench had its place in the bottom-most drawer of my desk, right next to the syringes that I had stolen from the Charité hospital. On that morning of 10 November, I checked to make sure that the wrench was still in its place. For the first time, I looked at it with personal interest. "I hope that I won't lose it again" was the thought that set in before I tried to continue playing the reasonable one. And I went to fetch the newspaper from the mailbox, since I couldn't have slept even if I tried.

16

After I had recovered from the initial shock of the Wall's collapse and had pulled myself out of my self-pity, in the subsequent weeks I started to become fully alert. I had no hope of talking with Emanuel about the consequences of the opened borders. I had played the role of the political simpleton, incapable of making any sort of political decision, for too long. Why should he believe me now, of all times? My cautious efforts at telling him that socialism was coming to an end here and now led repeatedly to unproductive arguments. In January 1990, when the first free elections to the People's Chamber (Volkskammer) were moved up from May to March, I gently tried to point out to Emanuel that he might also look after himself, in addition to the greater good. For one couldn't promote world revolution without eating now and again. He was beside himself with anger that I could be so egoistic at a time like this, which demanded everything, even me. He was right for the first time in years.

That very January I received anonymous phone calls that went: "Jew sow, Jew woman, out with the Jews." Always the same phrase, but spoken by different voices. We contacted the police. They tried to trace the calls, but without any success. People threw garbage and empty bottles at our front door. I felt threatened by the people's anger, which certainly was also connected with the apartment. I had heard that others who lived on our street were protesting the apartment's allocation to us, which we had received contrary to all the prevailing GDR regulations. Emanuel spoke about the mobs that always surfaced at such times and insisted that I not stay in the apartment alone. We decided that when he had to be out of town a male friend would come and stay with me. He would be able to protect me from the people's "healthy anger." After about two months this harassment stopped. This was the beginning of a learning process: what it meant to have been a part of the East German establishment.

Meanwhile, negotiations over German unification were taking place at the highest levels. The CDU won a triumphant victory in the elections to the People's Chamber* and this promoted the frenzy over a monetary union on the basis of the West German mark (or DM). Speculations over the conditions for the currency exchange – at the ratio of either 1:2 or 1:1 – encouraged money dealers to acquire East German currency. The selling off of the GDR on the domestic market gained momentum. Foreign traders had done this for years under the direction of Schalck-Golodkowski* – and in collusion with the Stasi. Now finally, under Lothar de Maizière's transitional administration,* East German citizens could do it too.

For all my astonishment about the historic events, I kept a certain distance from the democratic frenzy for reunification. This too stemmed from my experiences in West Berlin before the Wall had gone up: I knew that living in the free world cost money. My travels in the West had already reminded me of this fact. Remembering friends of my grandmother's, I travelled to Frankfurt am Main and Munich. I asked them what I should do now in order to exist as a writer in the Federal Republic, since – at least twenty years too late – I had to become a West German again. They advised me to get a literary agent and a good accountant. The latter was quickly found. A friend from my childhood in West Berlin had, after giving up her musical career, married a tax consultant. Together they ran a very successful tax consultancy in West Berlin. But she stayed in touch with the musical world, since she primarily attended to the Berlin Philharmonic's tax affairs. She promised to do everything she could as soon as the unification treaties allowed it. Later the entire Kuczynski family became her clients.

As for the literary agent, my grandmother's friends had given me a letter of introduction that led me to Switzerland. While still at home I purchased an answering machine, using some of the hundred DM that every East German received as "welcome money" from the free world. I arranged for an electrician from the East German telephone company to install it for me on the side, since what I wanted was illegal in both the East and the West. The West German Bundespost* did not authorize the use of low-cost machines made by Panasonic, and in East Germany, even in its dying days, it was forbidden to connect an answering machine. For a substantial fee, though, the electrician from the German Post made the connection possible. Now, by accessing the machine remotely, I could keep up with the activities of my freelance business at home. So I went to Switzerland. I introduced myself to the agent. It was love at first sight. And we became good friends in the years to come. She promised to take care of me, and she did.

The search for my own literary agent was the first independent act I took after the Wall opened. It did me good. I knew that living as a freelance writer in unified Germany would be next to impossible. Still, I had to try, for by then writing had become my way of life. It was my way of getting in touch with the world. Indeed, by then, my life depended on writing. Hence, I had no other choice but to try. I knew that I didn't have the energy to take on occasional jobs and then write on the side. The question that reverberated among all the other questions of the next few years was this: how can I create the necessary conditions for existing as a writer?

In the meantime, the Ministry of Culture had granted permission for my book, *Wenn ich kein Vögel wär*, to be published, without any requests for changes. The director of the publishing house cynically professed that he first needed the historical experience of the Wall's collapse to understand the novel, which told the "story of a childhood in divided Berlin." In the frenzy over unification, the book took on political significance, which also pushed the publisher to feature it at the Frankfurt Book Fair. The same happened with the film based on the book, in whose production two West German film studios immediately invested. Completed in late 1990/early 1991, it was DEFA's last feature film.

Thanks to the contracts for the film version of my book, I suddenly had a good deal of money. I was paid in East German marks for the entire film, including the instalments that hadn't yet been filmed before 1 July 1990. I didn't know what I should do with the money. There were money handlers who were buying East German marks in front of the Interhotels in order to trade them for West German marks at the ratio of 1:1 following the currency union. Since it was impossible to talk with Emanuel about practical things, I asked my father-in-law, who had some experience with such matters as money, currencies, and the global economy and who also wasn't changing social systems for the first time. He advised me to divide our money between our accounts so that neither one had an excessively high balance. Then, when the right moment came after the currency union, we should split up the funds and buy gold. For this practical sense, too, I loved him, despite his theoretical inclinations.

There was a peculiar mood in the country. The black market in cars, colour televisions, and video recorders flourished. From week to week, one sensed that the GDR was spinning out of control. The uncertainty and anxiety about what was coming produced some bizarre and sad reactions. One woman I encountered on the street, for instance, advised me to go and have all my teeth pulled before the currency union took effect so that I could still get dentures on East German terms. She was an elementary school teacher and had just done it herself. She was proud of her foresight. She believed that East German health care was the best in the world.

There were months of panic buying. In those weeks, even I bought all kinds of stuff, from good woollen fabric – which is still lying in the chest since I don't have the money for a seamstress – to shoes, which I never wore because they weren't comfortable enough and were already out of fashion in unified Germany. I bought vast amounts of vitamins, not suspecting that fresh fruit and vegetables would make them superfluous. My best find during that summer of 1990 was a bucket full of Ohropax earplugs from the pharmacy, for I was wise enough to foresee that it could get rather loud in the next few years. During my trips to the United States I had learned that I was allergic to most brands of earplugs and this sufficed to convince me that I couldn't have enough of these small pink balls. Even today, I still stop up my ears at night with that sticky Ohropax from the "People's Own" Ankerwerk Firm in Rudolstadt.

But it wasn't just the time of the GDR clearance sale, it was also a time for buying. The East German market became inundated with bananas and oranges as well as with unknown fruit like kiwis and mangos that I really didn't know how to prepare. The digestive problems from these fruits and vegetables became a sort of "transition sickness" for many East German citizens. And I was far from alone in buying charcoal tablets to deal with the diarrhea. A pharmacist offered to sell me under the table an enormous quantity of them for a special price. Two years ago, long after their expiration date, I disposed of these tablets along with other GDR-era medications at the same pharmacy. The pharmacist had gone into business for himself after unification.

In the meantime, I became politically active. I went to the authors' union and got involved in the discussion over the goals of a union that, in my opinion, should be first and foremost a professional association, not a lobby for propagandists and ideologues. Together with other writers we sought to fight against the GDR's contract writers and cultural bigwigs, and with some success. We set up committees to prepare for new union elections. And before I had taken a proper breath, I was on one of these election committees. Since I had studied the field of demagoguery longer than most other writers, I got involved in the discussions with the union's officials, the greater part of whom were later exposed as Stasi informants. Faced with the decision to be a candidate in the upcoming election to the executive committee for Berlin, I demurred. I didn't feel strong enough for the immense amount of work that would come my way. For the moment, though, I remained active in the union.

The work on the new novel faltered. Full of enthusiasm, I read books by Wolfgang Leonhard, Arthur Koestler, and Manès Sperber.* I realized that others had long known what I discovered in the months after the Wall's collapse: the real history of communism in the Soviet Union, the Moscow show trials. I read Koestler's novel, *Darkness at Noon*, many times over. I studied the logic of the confessions, the logic of people's readiness to sacrifice themselves, the logic of the voluntary submission of the individual to the Party's will, for, in the end, only someone free of individual will was a good comrade. And a good comrade believes in the Party, and in his faith he submits completely and totally to the Party. He believes before seeking to establish through reason what could not be established through reason but simply is. "Faith cannot acquired by empirical reasoning," I read in another of Koestler's works.* "Reason may defend an act of faith, but only after the act has been committed ... faith grows like a tree, it matures in realms where no persuasions can penetrate." All of a sudden I was happy that I had never succeeded in believing in the socialist cause, but also a bit melancholic, because I hadn't managed to believe in anything at all and remained godless, which meant that I alone was responsible for everything that I did or didn't do.

My game of hide and seek thus had consequences. I understood that very soon after the Wall fell. I was caught off guard. What I had pondered within my own four walls had long ago been thought through and was available in classic texts published in more than thirty languages. I read like an addict, but only bit by bit did it sink in that all of these books were in my father-in-law's library. I asked him why neither he nor Emanuel had ever mentioned it. He said, "Because you were possessed of a charming immaturity in political matters, and still are," and kissed me on the forehead. I could never be angry with him, but I made horrible scenes in front of Emanuel and showered him with senseless accusations. In the end, he had done just as I had done during the more than fifteen years of our marriage: he had kept to our express agreement not to discuss politics.

But circumstances had changed. The reason for my denial of politics no longer existed. I was no longer forcibly locked up. My resistance against the holy simplicity of political propaganda had lost its purpose. The socialist agitprop theatre with its standing program of making clear to me how lucky I was to be allowed to live confined behind the Wall had to discontinue its performances on account of bankruptcy. Therefore, I could also abandon my counter-program of political abstinence. Now I had a hunger for political information that couldn't be sated. I read spellbound Hannah Arendt's *The Origins of Totalitarianism*, paying particular attention to the chapter "Ideology and Terror: A Novel Form of Government," since it contained sentences that were very relevant to the mental place in which I had lived for over twenty years. It held insights into the historical fatalism that I had myself embraced, not suspecting that my behaviour was not original in the least, but rather the entirely normal progression of the pathology of forced confinement. Once more, I was on the verge of forgetting the world around me to study this text of Hannah Arendt.

I teetered between reading and real events. In the meantime, not only had the currency union occurred, but also unification. I attended my first book fair in Frankfurt am Main, where my novel *Wenn ich kein Vogel wär* was released on the Day of German Unity (3 October). I sat with friends – who were no longer my "West German" friends now but simply "friends" – in a Greek restaurant near St Paul's church eating olives and drinking red wine. When the bells in the city rang out and the blue and green fireworks soared, I was already somewhat anxious. I would have to make an effort to avoid becoming sentimental.

What happened next happened so quickly that I had difficulty understanding it. Between numbness and helplessness I heard how the time fell away, one era into another. I noticed how it lost its dimensions, since its structures were breaking into pieces. I was caught in a rhythm whose tempo accelerated from each break to the next. The time before and the time after in a present about which I did not understand that it was only disappearing. There was a vacuum and over-pressure at the same time. I hung in the air. There seemed to be no more ground. I didn't know how and where I could put my foot down. How would I keep my balance? While I concentrated on regaining my balance so that I did not fall headfirst, some west German feminists* asked me how I felt about all this as a woman. "Miserable," I answered. First my lover had returned to Chile, second my marriage was rapidly falling apart, and third I missed my flour. The western flour was all wrong: its consistency was either too thick or too thin. I couldn't make a good sauce with it any more.

This "I didn't understand" became a state of being. I tried to write about it by beginning to write my novel *Über die Kinder der roten Aristokratie* (About the Children of the Red Aristocracy). In the meantime I was aware that I was also one of them, whether I liked it or not. While I was writing, I ran out of salt. I had to learn that salt wasn't just salt, and bought one saltshaker after another. Their holes became smaller and smaller. Better to add less at first; after all, one can always add salt later – this was one of the first insights I had into the new era's range of options.

And while I heard ever more clearly how one era collapsed into another, there remained the open question of how I was going to earn a living. Emanuel drifted between his worries over the faltering world revolution and the fight to preserve his Institute at the Academy. To the end, he never believed that his Institute would be phased out. Asking him about such a banal matter as how to finance one's life was pointless.

And, in truth, even I found this question banal. Since my arrival in the GDR, I had never once posed it to myself. But now it stood insistently before me. I recalled that, in the first years after the Wall went up, I had lived primarily by stealing. To start with that again, however, seemed too risky. I didn't know much about the countless types of electronic anti-theft devices. Moreover, my reflexes were no longer as good as they had been twenty-eight years ago. I had swallowed too many sedatives in order to endure my socialist happiness. I still took them and anyway suffered from a lack of concentration in daily life, one of the side effects from all these pills. I thus resolved not to start stealing again. I only stole one single top from an expensive boutique. It was so easy that I vowed never to do it again and, up to now, I have been true to my word.

So, what was I going to live on? In East Germany one could live practically for free. That is, eating, living, and clothing hardly cost anything. One could get by with 400 East marks (*Ostmark*): it wasn't great, much less refined, but one could get enough. Everyone had a place to live: it wasn't great, but no one was lying in the street. People had clothes to wear: they weren't modern, but they were warm and occasionally even functional. One could subsist in East Germany without the "Delikat" and "Exquisit" stores, even without Intershops.* This experience, that the physical maintenance of life cost virtually nothing in East Germany, was one of the fundamental experiences from my time there. Even in my first years there, it had made a profound impression on me.

Today, many former East German citizens consider that the low cost of living in East Germany was a sign of the GDR's superiority. "Money wasn't a factor in our lives," they say. "That is the capital that we can bring to German unity." What was overlooked, though, was that in the end the GDR perished precisely because of this. It wasn't quite accurate to say that it didn't cost anything to live in East Germany. It actually cost quite a bit. And Schalck-Golodkowski wasn't the first to worry about Western money on the state's behalf, which most East Germans knew about only from the two West German public television channels, ARD and ZDF. Had socialism been capable of existing in isolation from the world market, it might have taken longer for it to collapse from its own economic inefficiencies. Within real existing socialism, the Law of Value could indeed be suspended by Party resolution, and from time to time it could be reintroduced by Party resolution, but the world market paid no heed to Party resolutions.

The nostalgic memory that money wasn't a factor in East Germany also wasn't true for real life in the GDR. It may well be that many East German citizens, like myself, didn't take the East mark seriously, dismissed Forum cheques for the Intershops as play money,* and only regarded West German currency, which they never got hold of, as real money. To that extent, money played in fact no role, not even for Schalck-Golodkowski, for he was concerned about foreign currency. And the state? It worried about interest-free overdraft credits from the Federal Republic. It worried about the daily rates charged to Wall tourists and about the "sale" of political prisoners to West Germany, one of the most questionable humanitarian "achievements" in the two Germanies' postwar history.

Looking back, it seems to me that this notion that money played no role in the GDR was really one of many self-deceptions, which also didn't take into account that, in East Germany, privileges were money. That applied especially to a social system based on privilege and personal relations of dependence, which in itself was hierarchically structured by privilege.

But much more important seemed to me the fact that, ten years after the GDR's collapse, some of its intellectuals still could not see that, through their choice of the "Alliance for Germany" in their first free election, East Germans voted for the D-Mark (the West German currency) as their currency precisely because the D-Mark was money with which they could buy something. In 1989 East German citizens left the suggestions for improving the world out in the cold, preferring by far money that had value. They ignored the second, third, and fourth paths to a better future and seized the historic offer of the day: the much longed for D-Mark. Naturally, many intellectuals expressed their disappointment with the people. In the major German news magazines they had opportunities to proclaim their disapproval of the East German people, who had chosen bananas and used cars rather than go looking for a third way to a "true future." In all their outrage over the earthly needs of the East German people, large numbers of these East German artists and VIPs at least often forgot one small detail: for the most part they had visas – if not a permanent one, in any case one valid for a limited period – and had been driving their Western autos for some time, precisely because they were artists loyal to the state to whom other rules applied than those for most East German citizens. They could legally import their Western cars into East Germany or they received their foreign cars either through one of the artists' unions or the Ministry of Culture. Now they were paying for their arrogance towards the needs of broad sectors of the population. The people no longer cared about their plans for improving the world. The gap between intellectuals and common people, which seemed to have disappeared in the November days of 1989, now became greater every year. The great majority of these East German intellectuals have today disappeared, and hardly anyone misses them.

17

How was I then to earn a living? I understood very soon that social privileges were also money. My 68er friends* shared with me the experiences they as intellectuals had gained with the West German welfare state since the mid-1970s. They explained to me that many of the transitional rules for east Germans were "special offers for German unity" that I absolutely had to exploit. The most important thing, they insisted, was to come under the social safety net. To do that, I would have to take advantage of the special provisions and declare myself an unemployed freelance writer. This was normally impossible in the Federal Republic, for artists there were considered independent contractors. Therefore, as soon as my literary fellowship ran out, I was to go to the employment bureau, which I duly did at the end of 1991 – just before these transitional rules expired. My friends, who were mostly sociologists, political scientists, and philosophers, patiently explained to me that the employment bureau wouldn't just hand me a job. I had a legal right to the bureau's services, they explained, and the civil servants who worked there were obligated to help me find appropriate work. One of the sociologists gave me a copy of the pamphlet "Guidelines for the Unemployed," which the Technical College for Social Work in Frankfurt am Main published and updated every two years, even to this day. She wasn't the only one, though, who urgently advised me to study the guidelines carefully so that I understood how the unemployment and social welfare system functioned. I took their advice seriously: so, alongside Wolfgang Leonhard's *Child of the Revolution* I now read the "Guidelines for the Unemployed."* The matter-of-fact way in which my west German sociologist friends, every one of them in their philosophy a product of the Frankfurt School,* dealt with the unemployment system made my entry into this métier all the easier. Soon I found myself sitting in the employment bureau. Because of my professional background, I had been directed to the waiting room for *Führungskräfte*, that is, management-level employees. The word reminded me of what these people were called in East Germany, namely *Führungskader* (or leadership elite). In GDR times I had successfully fought against being included among them. It turned out that my association of the two words was not off base. For here in the waiting room, ten years after retiring from the life of a philosopher, I again encountered many of my former colleagues from the Academy of Sciences' Institute for Philosophy. My spontaneous cry – "What are you all doing here?" – was rather inappropriate. Their responses were spare and grudging. They were in turns embarrassed about being there, depressed that the Institute for Marxist-Leninist Philosophy had been shut down, and angry about German unification. I tried to steer the conversation to more neutral ground. I asked whether they already had their employment bureau account numbers and joked over the connotations of the new bureaucratic language we had to learn. When I noticed that that hadn't eased the tension, I returned to reading the second volume of Wolfgang Leonhard's book.

My transition to a free life in the Federal Republic was enormously facilitated by the fact that I had ceased being a salaried scholar ten years before the GDR fell apart. I was long since accustomed to working without assignments from a state institution. Even the fact that I never became an official GDR writer made my transition somewhat easier, since I didn't believe in my own social significance. For a long time, too, I had developed an ironic distance towards what I could achieve. Not that I hadn't taken my work seriously. But, just as I had always compared my philosophical contribution to that of other philosophers, at least in the history of European thought, so did I now compare my writing to that of other authors of world literature and knew that my contribution was rather modest.

Once more, I realized I would have to take responsibility for my own life. With Emanuel or alone, for the family's power wouldn't be able to protect him from the harsh facts of life much longer. Soon he too would have to move on, either alone or with me. I seriously doubted that we could pull it off together. The distance between us had grown too large. We did what we actually both hated: we argued without clearing up anything. We quarrelled over stupid things. The situation at home was stressful for both of us. To gain even more distance, I flew to Chile. But

I also left to say good-bye to Claude and flew to a country whose dictatorship had just been abolished. Besides, I had promised to come as soon as it was possible. During the flight I toyed with the idea of staying in Chile. Perhaps I could find work at the university. In the GDR's final years, I had discovered the Chilean poet and Nobel Prize winner Gabriela Mistral. I loved her poems for their sadness and their simplicity. I had translated umpteen poems by her into German and studied how they came about. Furthermore, I knew many Chileans in Santiago itself, in addition to Claude, who could help me gain a foothold there.

Claude picked me up at the airport. I stayed at his house in La Reina. But the Claude I met again in 1991 wasn't the Claude from Berlin. Perhaps I had changed too much myself, had become more independent and freer in my power of judgment. Perhaps I had put into perspective the father figure that Claude, now fifteen years older, still was for me. Or maybe I just couldn't get over my disappointment, that – after all our years together – he hadn't included me at all in his decision to return to Chile, which he announced one morning out of the blue.

For days Claude and I walked on the ocean beach. We walked from Valparaíso to Viña del Mar and back. We drove to Antofogasta via La Serena. At the edge of the desert we sat down and were silent. After seven days and seven nights we stood up and again and decided to return home: Claude to Santiago and I to Berlin. I wanted to try starting over with Emanuel.

Too late. Emanuel had found someone else, a comrade. He now wanted to fight on with her. I tried as best I could to win back my husband. Too late. We separated from one another and Emanuel went looking for his own apartment.

I unpacked my starfish. We had dried them on the beach in the sun, Claude and I. For weeks still, they stank of rotten fish and attracted flies. I sorted out the mussel shells and placed them in a glass bowl. After that I lay down in bed. I didn't ever want to get up again.

So now there I was in my six-room apartment. It was supposed to be my castle behind the Wall. If I had struggled to acquire this apartment in the first place, I would now have to struggle to hold on to it. The rent had already been raised for the first time, and one could expect that further increases would follow. I had rented the 200-square-metre (2150-square-foot) apartment for 172 *Ostmark*. Soon I was paying seven times that; today I pay more than ten times that amount. In the meantime, virtually all of the stately tenants moved out. In their place came families with many children, whose rent was paid by the social welfare bureau. For the time being, I decided not to give up the apartment. I desperately wanted to have a fixed point to which I could return amidst all the upheaval that was occurring and for which there was no end in sight. I had the idea that if I gave up this apartment, I would lose a very important point of reference to myself. It was the first apartment that I had anything to do with, because, from its very foundation, it reminded me of my grandmother's house. In this apartment I wanted to provide a place for my existence as a writer. To give this place up at that moment was tantamount to capitulating. So began the odyssey of finding lodgers. The rent rose more and more. I soon realized that only west Germans could afford to rent two rooms in my apartment. The rooms were simply too expensive for people with east German salaries. Here too my 68er friends helped me.

My first lodger was a pastor from West Berlin, who wished to bring the Christian faith to East Berlin and other new parts of the Federal Republic. He played the violin, which was a treat for me, since he played quite well. Now and then he also played the piano, albeit with less professionalism. Bach's cantatas and masses, though, he sang to himself quite acceptably and in accordance with the church calendar. Occasionally I joined him in singing. Then both of us went humming through the apartment. That sufficed as communication between us.

Meanwhile, the "literary fame" surrounding my book, *Wenn ich kein Vogel wär*, had died down. So too the publicity surrounding the film based on it, which by then had had its premiere. I was forced to learn that, as a media and cultural event, a book has a lifespan of about six weeks. The question of how I was to earn a living, thus, stood blatantly before me again. My father-in-law was quite worried about me, then in particular; after Emanuel moved out, he stood by me continually until his own death. On various occasions, he insisted that if I couldn't keep my apartment any longer, I could move in with them. Two rooms in his house would always be available for me. I really appreciated his support. And the idea of having two rooms in his house calmed me, even if I could never claim them. My relationship with the rest of the family was deteriorating and their jealousy and their envy over the ever more affectionate relationship between me and my father-in-law only grew, especially once Emanuel and I separated. My father-in-law made no secret of his affection and he was glad that I had managed to publish in the Federal Republic. He still didn't read what I wrote, nor did I read what he published. But about every eight weeks he came by with flowers, if, in the meantime, I hadn't visited him and brought him flowers, taking the opportunity to tell him about what I was writing and how far along I was with my next book. He was very pleased that I was moving forward on my own and he collected even the shortest notice about me from the newspapers to give to me.

I had accepted work in an agency for female journalists. It was a job creation measure and most closely resembled occupational therapy, albeit one that paid quite well. I was supposed to write a philosophical work on feminist theories in the Federal Republic. It was my first contact with "our people" in over twenty years. Over the months that I worked there I acquired a vague notion of how high, intellectually too, I had flown over the real conditions of life under socialism. Most of the women who worked there had come from the socialist newspaper and illustrated magazine business. They had studied journalism in Leipzig or had just finished a degree in German language and literature. They were all under thirty and true children of the GDR who lost their jobs when the GDR collapsed. They knew the West only from television or the papers. Having grown up behind the Wall, they had that generation's advantage of not being plagued by the mental shortcomings of the educated middle classes' convictions. They went forth fresh and carefree and disregarded the traditions of their cultural heritage: therein lay this generation's enormous creative opportunity. However, if they lacked creativity, this same disregard became a disadvantage, especially when coupled with the socialist educational system's provincial narrowness.

During the months I worked there, but also in the months thereafter, I realized that by living in a Jewish family with atheist beliefs, as I had done for nearly twenty years, I had long ago left the GDR, intellectually too. The family's worldliness and the worldliness of the Jewish intellectuals with whom I had been in conversation for years had left their mark on me. I had been integrated into their cultural sphere. I loved their humour, their jokes, and their sadness. I loved their intellectualism, which usually was also mixed with mischief and irony. Even today I am sometimes amazed by German intellectuals' often unflinching resistance – in the West and in the East – to irony, and by their lack of humour. For this reason, too, I strengthened the intellectual contacts with my Jewish friends, who lived mainly in the United States and in England.

Time was speeding up in a way I had never experienced before. I refused to adopt its tempo. I tried to resist it by setting up my own standards. I tried to find a rhythm so that the pace with which everything around me was proceeding would not crush me. Indeed, my problem was to avoid being crushed by what I called "the rush of events." With all my might I tried to resist the maelstrom into which I had been caught up, as one time collapsed into another. I concentrated, or rather, I tuned myself to a fundamental tone so I didn't get lost. From this I wanted to devise a melody that could carry me through the rupture. Hence, in the middle of all my activities I paused over and over and listened to see if I could still hear the tone. For I knew that if I didn't hear it, I ran the risk of falling again into the bottomless pit. But going crazy was pretty much the only thing I didn't want. So I stopped when, instead of my melody, I heard voices piercingly high in the wind. They were the same ones that I heard twenty-eight years ago after the Wall had been built. This time too they spoke of how I at least needed to abandon my pride in order to find my happiness in the herd, and finally surrender, surrender …

"Thinking is action": I had lived this fundamental proposition of classical German philosophy in the GDR. I wanted to be as inconspicuous as possible so that in my preferred place – my study – I could find tranquillity and concentrate on my texts. The black dresses and the scarves that I wore over the years; the long hair, behind which I could hide my face; the sedative tablets that I took to deal with my anxiety and my lack of self-control, which I quit calling spontaneity long ago – these were also part of it. For again and again spontaneity had made my life in the GDR unbearably difficult. I couldn't break out laughing, for laughter always aroused suspicion, couldn't explode, even when I was so inclined. A certain dosage of diazepam provided me a remedy against both. Having learned that a new generation of tranquillizers was discovered every ten years, I managed to time things so that I moved from one generation to the next before my body had developed a resistance to the active ingredient then available on the market. The last newly developed generation of tranquillizers, which hit the market around 1987 – albeit not yet in East Germany – was obtained for me by my lover through a doctor in Paris, and later from Chile, until the fall of the Wall let me have the joy of obtaining the prescription for myself in Germany.

In addition to depression, taking these tablets also caused a significant retardation of my capacity to react. In the present "now time" this was anything but practical, since the ability to make quick decisions and keep a clear head was now essential. There was constantly something to decide, and new demands kept coming. During the first two or three years after the Wall fell, I thought that this would all pass, just as any exceptional situation did, and that afterward everything would return to normal. Now and then during these first years after the Wall collapsed, I thought that I was sitting in a theatrical production that at some time or another would finally come to an end. It took a while before I understood that, in fact, the twenty-eight years behind the Wall had been one long exceptional situation, no matter how much I had settled into it.

Since the agony of making all these decisions didn't subside, I decided to wean myself off the tablets. Slowly phasing them out was my plan. Since for months now I barely slept, I worked on my novel about the children of the red aristocracy at night, which I now called *Im Kreis* (In the Circle). It was the story of Esther and me and my life within the "first security circle," as I dubbed the lifestyle of the East German nomenklatura.

In the meantime, my lodger, the pastor, had moved out. He had found an "East German wife," as he proudly put it. They wanted to move into their own apartment together. So once again I faced the problem of finding a lodger. This time I offered the room to the Berlin Senate as a luxury apartment in the East. Shortly after the local officials inspected my apartment, the first civil servant was referred to me. He worked in the Federal Labour Office, was twenty-three years old, and came from Stuttgart. He was supposed to train his "new German" colleagues out in Berlin-Marzahn, a socialist development district during the GDR era.* He earned a lot of money for this; after all, he was carrying out redevelopment work in the new German regions, as he later professed to me without any irony.

Well, brilliant, I thought, now I have the employment bureau in my apartment too. I took care not to tell him that I was unemployed just now. I introduced myself to him as a freelance writer, which was accurate, only that when no royalties or stipends were coming in, I reported myself as unemployed.

At the time when I took on this first civil servant from the Federal Labour Office as a lodger, I was still writing my novel *Im Kreis*. I was still weaning myself off my pills and hardly slept. The young man from Stuttgart was very impressed with my obsessive work habits. Since he didn't have the slightest clue that I was legally unemployed, he used me as a positive example in his counselling at the employment bureau in Berlin-Marzahn, where he was in charge of providing employment advice to "managerial staff" and artists. He said that if you really wanted to, you could manage it. He remarked that for over half a year he had been living at an artist's who worked almost night and day and, consequently, she also pulled it all off. When he told me this in the kitchen, I cast down my eyes and thanked God, whom I could not believe in, that he hadn't said my name at the employment bureau. That evening we drank a bottle of red wine together. As we talked, I made up the story of Kati, a poor artist who wanted to set up her own business. I asked him if he knew what would be the most sensible way for her to proceed in order to receive bridge money from the employment bureau at good terms. To help my poor artist friend, he then provided me with the text of the most recent regulations concerning the Labour Promotion Act and its special regulations for East Germany. And long after he had returned to Stuttgart, he continued to send me these regulations.

His successor worked at the employment bureau where I was registered. Thankfully, I had received a fellowship just before he moved in with me. Hence, I had sufficient time to find out exactly where he sat so that I wouldn't run into him at the bureau. For at some point, the fellowship would run out. But until then I would have enough time to learn when he planned to take his long weekend – and that would be my opportunity to go to the employment bureau without him seeing me. I soon knew that on the fourth Friday of every month he had "home leave," as he put it. I could thus coordinate my visits to the employment bureau with his home leave. With him, too, I feared mentioning that I was unemployed. For as an employee of the Federal Labour Office, he might get the idea that I was misusing my unemployment benefits – at the apartment it was impossible to hide the fact that I didn't just work at night, but also during the day, that is, during the time that I was supposed to be available for work arranged by the employment bureau. An official there had explained that, as a writer and a philosopher, I was not allowed to write books during the hours I was supposed to place my labour at the employment bureau's disposition. When I asked to which hours that rule applied, he replied: from eight in the morning until four in the afternoon. And so, whenever I received royalty payments, I reported them with the written comment that the royalties were for work that I had written outside of normal working hours, thereby staying within the terms of the Federal Labour Office's regulations.

I thus had managed to make provisional arrangements for myself that, for the time being, permitted me to continue writing. The shuttling back and forth between royalties, stipends, and employment bureau benefits had reached an initial state of normality and routine. The conditions were not ideal, but they offered me the concentration I needed to write. When I could no longer make ends meet financially, I sold my first editions of classic German philosophy texts. It was a fad to collect them in GDR times, but it had also been essential to scholarly activity, since newer editions of many classic philosophical texts were never published in East Germany – Hegel's *Philosophy of Religion*, for example. It was published for the first time in the summer of 1989.

18

A certain sense of normality also established itself in the day-to-day interactions between the former East and West Germans. The pace of the historical breakdown had lost speed. Three, four years of German unity had spread through the land. The idea had taken hold, and not just among my west German friends, that they had personally played a part in the recent historical events. They felt that they had made some sort of contribution to German unity. One philosopher of religion went to the heart of the matter when she proclaimed: "We have won the war." Somewhat astonished, I asked her which war, and it turned out that she meant the Cold War. So among my 68er friends, too, a national "we feeling" had developed concerning the victory over the East Germans. Inexplicably, even my 68er friends understood themselves to be winners in a historical process that had proceeded without them and for which they had done nothing, absolutely nothing at all. They were not only particularly surprised that the socialist world system had collapsed behind their backs. They were also shocked that their socialist ideals gave way on the other side of the Wall, the Wall that they had only crossed, when at all, to celebrate Aunt Elfriede's birthday or to see a play at the Berliner Ensemble.* After they had recovered from the shock that something had again occurred in the real world that they had not predicted – the real collapse of East Germany as the fictional location of their socialist utopias – they exploited the historical opportunity of the hour. They styled themselves as victors.

Not for nothing had I managed their "exchange money," which they had to pay to visit the socialist state circus in East Berlin, and bought for them over the years the complete works of Marx, Engels, and Lenin. There my 68er friends had found the key passages concerning class warfare and the possibilities for their demagogic interpretation.

Communication became more difficult for us. In the discussion that such overblown ideas made unavoidable, I learned that I was now one of the losers and therefore had to learn from them.

I learned, too, that our ties of friendship had been spatially determined. The Wall had been their foundation. Me here, them there – that was the cement of our friendship. Our encounters resembled encounters with extraterrestrials: when we met, they told me of their world, which I knew only from hearsay, and I told them about mine, which they knew only from stories. Unable to communicate to each other the differences in our lived experiences, we developed a sense of closeness. Surprised by the GDR's collapse, though, we were now suddenly sitting together in one world. The "there" had disappeared. The relationship of equals, the precondition for our friendship, had disappeared. The Wall's collapse had buried it. On its rubble grew the obsession with "the victors of history" with which my 68er friends, feeling historically superior, now approached and obligingly lectured me.

Fortunately, thanks to my years among the hero-children, I already had some experience with living among the victors of history. I discontinued political discussions with my historically superior friends. When I met with them, I focused instead on daily life. And there was a lot to learn. Eventually, nothing in my kitchen was as it had been in GDR times. Milk no longer turned sour. Meat no longer tasted like meat. Expiration dates on canned foods were no longer reliable, whereas in East Germany food had usually been safe for as long as two years. Furthermore, I learned that one didn't eat canned goods when fresh fruit and vegetables were available. I learned how to buy vegetables at the market and tell one kind of eggplant from another, as well as how to prepare it – either by itself or with zucchini. I learned how to eat kiwis and mangos and sort through the enormous options for noodles that, I found out, had always been called pasta. From one of my psychologist friends I learned that I overdid things when cleaning the bathroom and toilet and had a nearly obsessive desire for cleanliness – which were clearly connected to my years in East Germany. I discovered that one cleaning agent was enough for the entire house. I learned how to tell if it was phosphate-free and, hence, environmentally friendly, and that one didn't buy spray cans containing chlorofluorocarbons. I learned, too, that one didn't grow petunias in the flower boxes on the kitchen windows, but rather rosemary, lemon balm, and basil.

Thus, by applying one of the 68ers' most important theses – the private is the political – to our daily encounters, friendly interaction with them remained possible. Moreover, I was quickly learning the standards of everyday life in western Germany, which I no longer wanted to do without.

After I too was aware of preservatives in cheese and sausage and had understood why one didn't drink ultra-pasteurized milk, we started to run out of things to talk about, since I refused to assume the part of the loser and the mentally handicapped any longer. After the GDR's collapse, the thought of continuing to play the fool seemed absurd to me. I also saw no reason suddenly to gather together justifications for my life in East Germany. My psychologist friend viewed my stubborn behaviour as a symptom of repression. She was worried about me. I could live with that. Intellectually, I could run with the very best in what had been West Germany. As far as I could tell from what I had seen of the social sciences and humanities in West Germany, dilettantism, activism, and scholarly accomplishment coexisted together there just as they did elsewhere. My impression was that the social scientists were less rigorous in their thinking than were the humanists. But then, the social scientists, especially those who called themselves "leftists," had more political debris from the Cold War era to clear away. The humanists, it seemed to me, had a more solid disciplinary training. And, as a philosopher, I felt closer to them because of their ways of thinking.

In the meantime, a female journalist again asked me how I was faring as a woman. I admit that, after living German unity for four years as a single woman, I understood her question differently now. "Badly," I replied. "First, I find it outrageous that people try to persuade me that, at the age of fifty, there are no more career opportunities for me. According to the official jargon, I was 'difficult to place.' Second, I find it intolerable that dissatisfied husbands want to cry on my shoulder and think that they are somehow also doing me a favour. Moreover, that men even in their nineties believe that they are irresistible, simply because they belong to the species 'man,' is equally unbearable." Why so many women put up with the macho behaviour and disrespect – I've been thinking about that now for some time.

It was now three years since Emanuel had moved out. After almost twenty years of marriage, I still hadn't got used to living alone. Either I cooked too much, or not at all. I didn't know how to shop for just one person and was constantly throwing food away.

Now and then I saw Emanuel, largely because through taxes, the revenue office, and the housing association we were bureaucratically still connected. Besides, it took us a while before we both gave up the habit of discussing intellectual problems with one another. From time to time, each of us made tentative efforts at getting back together. But there was no going back. The wounds we had inflicted on each other were too deep. Emanuel couldn't understand that I had only stayed in the East for his sake. He didn't find it at all flattering. To the contrary, he was appalled. Over the years, he had been under the illusion that I had recognized that socialism was, at least historically, the better alternative. Therefore, after the Wall collapsed, I was also obligated to work for its preservation. For my part, I couldn't understand why he, as a scholar, didn't contribute to intra-German unity after 1989. Or why he didn't write about the large distortions in and collapse of the socialist world system. After all, for years he had studied crisis cycles – both historical and contemporary ones. Now, with a crisis right there on the street, he was in a position to experience them personally on a daily basis. But he was interested neither in crises nor their cycles. Instead of being fascinated that life was showing him how a crisis could set a society in motion, he felt himself personally offended by the historical rupture and ceased his scholarly activity. I just couldn't understand it, or more specifically, I couldn't forgive him that all his scholarly interests were political ones. The fundamental compromise in our relationship couldn't be revived under the new social conditions. It took some time before we both finally realized this. And it took some time before I could cope, to some extent, with everyday life on my own.

I discovered my interest in technology. Soon after Emanuel had moved out, I bought myself a new computer. It made me profoundly insecure that Emanuel would no longer be able to proofread what I wrote, since I tend to make lots of careless mistakes when writing. The idea of using a spell-checking program calmed me, even if I soon had to accept that it was inadequate. I held on to my first computer, which I had brought back from the United States with me in 1987, for quite some time, partly because I was attached to it, but also because it was a souvenir of the trip to the United States that had such enduring consequences for my life. However, I wrote my novel *Im Kreis* on the new computer from the first to the last line. I didn't understand my 68er friends' reservations about technology. Their arguments about how the use of electronics in everyday life was increasingly alienating us from our humanity seemed absurd to me, given everything that microelectronics were making possible. My 68er friends' technophobia reminded me of a debate among the early German romanticists circa 1800. Then they criticized the rise of "big industry" by saying that true human relations were being destroyed by machinery. I was very pleased with inventions of modern electronics and considered the work that the computer accomplished for me as an immense relief.

The novel *Im Kreis* was finished by the end of 1994. My Swiss agent shopped the manuscript. The results were sobering: no publisher wanted the book. My agent was disappointed after several publishers had turned down my new book. I asked her to send me the rejections, insofar as she had received them in writing. I was irritated, not by the rejections themselves, but rather by the consensus in the German publishers' reasons for rejecting the manuscript. There was a noticeable similarity in their arguments' logic, which I had not suspected. It was all bound up with ideological views.

When the East German publishers rejected my book *Wenn ich kein Vogel wär*, one of the publishers (which has since been bought out) wrote: "... Unfortunately the author hasn't succeeded in her thoroughly praiseworthy effort to deal with the post-1953 era, that is, the period following Stalin's death. The behaviour of the novel's female protagonist is indecisive and emotionally incomprehensible, and consequently unclear in her commitment to the GDR ... At the press we ... have in mind a discussion of this complex historic period, during which the construction of a socialist society occurred, that is more partisan, that is, more socialist, and thereby more realistic, more based on the historical facts." That was 1986, place: East Berlin.

I laid these rejections next to those my agent had sent me for *Im Kreis*. In one letter the reviewer wrote: "I find the allegorical form of Rita Kuczynski's manuscript not modern enough for, say, discussing an authoritarian state. In any case, I believe that here at the press we must find other forms for presenting this sort of discussion." That was 1994, in unified Germany.

I let the reviewers' reports from the east and west German publishers lie on my desk for a few weeks. Internally, I struggled against making the generalization that, on both sides, the German spirit faced the same dilemma. I accepted that I belonged neither here nor there. Even in unified Germany, I would have to continue, unwillingly, going my own way.

To get a break from conditions in Germany, I applied for fellowships to the United States, receiving one from the Council for European Studies at Columbia University in New York. I read from my book *Im Kreis*. I gave lectures on censorship in German literature. I travelled across the

States with the new novel. On the fifth anniversary of German unification, I walked with a good friend from Buffalo over the US-Canadian border to see Niagara Falls from the Canadian side and eat ice cream. I was glad to be far away from Germany. I would have to think about how and where I could find the strength to go my own way even under the new conditions. During my trip, I learned how to use email. I was fascinated by the idea that I could be connected to friends at any time through the computer and the internet. The possibility of retrieving information from around the world via the internet and participating in worldwide discussion forums, and all this from my study in Berlin, was brilliant. Here again I didn't understand my 68er friends' concerns, who feared that I was being Americanized.

There was no reunion with Esther in the United States. Her husband, the rabbi, would not let me stay with them. I was frustrated, for I really wanted to experience Esther in "her America." Two days after my arrival in New York, I received a call from him saying that I couldn't come. It won't work, he said, she wasn't feeling well; moreover, there were the Jewish High Holy Days. How far apart from one another had we drifted? I travelled across the United States and read from her novel, which was also the story of our friendship. For a second time I said good-bye to Esther. This time it was definitive. "Sometimes the end is the end and nothing more," I wrote on a piece of a paper that I placed in my suitcase. I spent the Jewish High Holy Days with Jewish friends and their families and afterwards rebooked my flights.

With a notebook full of email addresses, I returned to Berlin and obtained a fax-modem. I thanked my friends in the United States via email for the good times that we had had together and for their hospitality. I was pleased to be connected with them now worldwide via the internet.

Five years after unification, intra-German sensitivities had increased. This struck me again after my long absence from the German arena. Five years after German unification, certain things had grown together that would have been better not to have grown together: the east German inferiority complex about having had the wrong currency their entire lives, which merged with the real helplessness that followed the GDR's collapse, where employment was not just secure but required by law. The mentality of someone who had missed out on life – which many east Germans displayed in their daily behaviour towards their west German brothers and sisters – did not diminish after the Wall fell, it increased. It was no longer about tax-deductible care packages, but rather about "solidarity contributions" and the flow of German marks from west to east.* In the years after unification, east Germans learned that the solidarity contribution was a benefit to which they were entitled; it was a just demand that they learned to justify. For had the territories east of the Elbe and, with them, some seventeen million east Germans not been sacrificed to the Soviets fifty years ago in order to make free development in the Trizone area possible,* the west German brothers and sisters never would have had it so good. Where the west Germans didn't accept their obligation to make amends, the east Germans' behaviour turned aggressive.

During the five years of unification, however, the idea had also set in among many west German intellectuals that what they had been doing for fifty years was correct; in fact, it was the only correct course of action. That they had for decades been receiving lessons in democracy from their own military occupiers, through which a half-decent constitutional state came into existence, was historically irrelevant. Like most fortunate children, they never questioned the source of their fortune, but made generalizations rather freely and, in the process, forgot the lessons in democracy and constitutional government that they had received from the occupying powers.

But it wasn't just among west Germans that the contours of history shifted. In their search for identity, many east Germans mixed up the sequence of historical events. It was thus no longer possible for them to shake the notion that they had been conquered by the west Germans. In their eyes, East German socialism hadn't collapsed because it went bankrupt along with the entire socialist world system, but rather because the GDR had been consumed by the Federal Republic. Accordingly, Treuhand – the privatization agency that took control over virtually the entire economy of a still formally existing socialist state in the spring of 1990 – became the starting point of East Germany's bankruptcy. In the eyes of many east Germans, Treuhand became the evil spirit that dumped East German firms on the world market after the socialist bloc's collapse. The fact that these firms were no longer worth anything following the socialist world system's collapse was never noticed. This is not to say that there were no instances of fraud and waste at Treuhand. But the historical sequence was: first the GDR collapsed economically, then Treuhand took over the insolvent assets of some eight thousand firms and four million workers because, among other reasons, the East Germans had freely chosen to become part of the Federal Republic.

Naturally, the pressure to adapt lay initially with the east Germans. But the reasons for the GDR's collapse, first and last, had nothing to do with East Germany and nothing at all with the former West Germany. They stemmed rather from the collapse of the socialist world system – in which the GDR was always just a member state. When east Germans sometimes behaved as if they had only just now arrived in an occupation zone, they were ignoring the fact as well that the socialist community of states had been smashed by the contributions of microelectronics to globalization.

Coping with this very globalization will soon force all Germans to give evidence of their capacity to adapt. Now here, compared with the west Germans, the east Germans have a considerable head start because of their history. That nothing will remain as it once was is something they have experienced, occasionally with great pain and suffering. West Germans thus will soon have the opportunity to demonstrate to all the world their own adaptability and mobility, which they often – and rightly – find missing in east Germans.

I had thus returned to the German arena and to the intra-German wrangling, which I found so difficult to fit into. I had never had a so-called East German identity and, for me at least, it just didn't work to invent one for myself after the fact. After the Wall fell, I broke away from my old 68er friends more than I had expected. In the search for my identity, I began to write a new novel. My female psychologist friends thought that I was incapable of learning. After my novel *Im Kreis* was rejected by publishers, they believed, I would finally have to accept that it couldn't go on like this. I should finally give up writing books, they meant; after all, I couldn't earn a living from it.

All the same, I had learned so much already that I had realized what I needed in order to live. It sounded too dramatic to come out and say that writing was my life. Since no fellowships and no royalties were in sight, I once again registered myself as unemployed and started writing a new novel. At the same time, I didn't forget to report to the employment bureau regularly in order to declare my availability for work anywhere in the world.

Since the east German staff in the employment bureaus had, in the meantime, learned the ropes of the unemployment "business" well enough that they could now manage things alone, the number of western civil servants coming to Berlin was decreasing. The Senate inspired little hope that I would have new lodgers, since its reconstruction assistance program was about to end. Rents were still going up in East

Berlin. I really had only two choices: either continue to take in lodgers or move. I didn't feel strong enough to move. I had still had times when I wasn't sure that what had happened and was still happening wasn't part of a larger stage production, only one where I didn't know which act I was in or what role I had in the play, whose title I also did not know. Hence, at least the apartment should be a place that, by force of habit, remained familiar to me.

Precisely because I was uncertain about which play I was in, I had to invent my own. A "play" in which I could appear, day after day, so that I could keep going. So I invented characters; I gave them names, which they accepted. I contrived a place where we met, day after day. Soon the characters became independent. They contradicted each other and insisted on having their own lives. Soon I only needed to listen very carefully in order to write down what they said and what they did. The novel practically wrote itself. From my experience with writing, I knew that this was a good sign.

While I worked on the novel, I had rented some rooms to the Goethe-Institute. But I was so engrossed in my text that I forgot about the renters. So sometimes I got irritated with the goings-on in my apartment. I encountered female students in the hallway; they politely said hello to me. Exhausted from jogging and with sweatbands on their foreheads, they walked past me into their bathroom and placed their white sneakers on the windowsill. From time to time they inquired whether they were allowed to use the kitchen or if, exceptionally, I might look over their homework. I didn't always know where they were from or what they were doing, but I did know that these well-behaved girls from Yale University or Oxford University didn't belong in my novel. For the characters in my novel had stumbled, been thrown off course by life and had to experience the world from its rough side. They lived on society's margins and, in order to survive, had banded together as a "self-help group for late resettlers," that is, ethnic German immigrants from Eastern Europe.

The novel was finished more quickly than I had thought. I forbade myself to think about what would happen if it weren't published. Ingeborg Bachmann's words about writing ran through my head:* "It is a strange, peculiar type of existence – asocial, solitary, damned, yes there is something cursed about it; and only what is published, the books, become social, associable, and find their way to 'you.'" I was afraid of letting this novel out of my hands, after my experience with the last one. But I had to do it. In the meantime, my Swiss agent had become seriously ill. She was in her eighties anyhow, which her exuberant way of life had made me forget. I gave the manuscript to a new agent. She didn't even need a month before she had found a publisher for my novel, *staccato*. That was in October 1996. The novel was to be released in March 1997 for the spring book fair, and it was.

After a portion of my royalties had arrived in my bank account, I went to the employment bureau to declare that I was returning to self-employed activity as a writer. It was likely that two or three hours would pass before my number would flash on the green illuminated display above the door. As always, I had brought plenty of reading material with me to keep me sensibly occupied during the endless waiting period. The stale air in the room and the monotonous sing-song with which the display illuminated the current queue number and the number of the room where the visitor was to go – all this made me sleepy. And for a few seconds I had in fact gone to sleep and forgotten the waiting room in which I was sitting. In any event, I brought back a sentence from out of this half-sleep, which I immediately wrote down: "I'm not yet on the street, the street lies before me!" The longer I played with this sentence in my head, the more clearly I heard a melody rise up that then developed into a composition. It was in the key of F major. I heard the entire composition. The longer I heard it, the more the tones were striving towards each other. They wanted to be connected. Such a connected style of delivery is called "legato." Beat for beat, I dropped into my memory in order to retain what I heard. I knew that what I heard was the basic tonal principle for a new novel. I wrote down a few sequences as well as a few variations on them. Then I put the slip of paper in my purse.

Once the employment bureau duly recorded my declaration that I would resume self-employed activity, I went home and wrote down what I had heard onto music paper. I laid the sheet on my desk. Then I retrieved my supply of phenobarbital, a narcotic sleeping aid, from the bottom-most drawer of the same desk. My lover had it sent to me from Chile and its expiration date had passed while I was working on *staccato*. I couldn't dispose of it at the pharmacist's, since I had over fifty grams of it. There would have been questions about where I had obtained it. I carried the poison to the garbage container for household waste.

"The notes are to be played one after another in a continuous, uninterrupted line," I read in a musical dictionary. I heard the "legato" from my composition again. To transpose it from music into a story would take me another two years.

NOTES

The numerals introducing each explanatory note refer to the page where the word or phrase occurs.

3 That is, the Second World War. Kuczynski uses the phrase to contrast the war years with the "Cold War" that followed.

4 Colloquial terms for, respectively, a Russian or an African-American soldier.

5 Formally inaugurated in 1930, the S-Bahn (or Stadtschnellbahn) is the rapid rail system that runs in and around Berlin (as contrasted to the city's system of elevated and underground lines, Berliner Hoch- und Untergroundbahnen, which is more commonly known as the U-Bahn).

6 In German, the Christliche Demokratische Union (or CDU), which became the main conservative party in the German Federal Republic (both before and after 1989).

6 The Sozialistische Einheitspartei Deutschlands (or SED) resulted from the forced union in 1946 of the Social Democratic and Communist parties in the part of Germany occupied by the Soviet Union. Until the regime's collapse in 1990, the SED was the sole ruling party in East Germany (formally, the German Democratic Republic or GDR).

6 "Baggi" is a made-up word, a bit of "kid-speak," as it were.

6 The Vineta Strasse subway line is now known as the U2; the Stadtmitte station is located in the heart of central Berlin ("Mitte"), only a few blocks away from what became the famed "Checkpoint Charlie" border crossing between East and West Berlin. However, only diplomats and military personnel could use Checkpoint Charlie; everyone else had to make use of one of the seven other crossings (which one depended on the mode of travel and one's place of origin).

6 A major industrial suburban area in the late nineteenth and early twentieth centuries, Pankow was formally incorporated into Berlin in 1920. Located north of the central city area and directly on the border with West

Berlin, it was one of East Berlin's most important neighbourhoods between 1949 and 1990 (and site of the East German president's official residence in the former Niederschönhausen Castle).

7 Within Communist Party circles, East Germany was referred to as the "Arbeiter- und Bauern-Staat," that is, the Workers' and Peasants' State.

8 HO and Konsum were the names of two major East German retail chains. The HO (for "Handelsorganization," that is, commercial society) was founded as a state enterprise in 1948 and was a kind of general store for consumer goods; its branches were found only in urban areas. The Konsum brand was founded in 1949, following the re-legalization of the consumer cooperatives (they had been dissolved during the National Socialist era); its stores were essentially grocery markets, present in both urban and rural settings.

8 The Schlachtensee is a lake that lies in the southwestern part of Berlin.

10 *Winterreise* (*Winter Journey*), is one of Franz Schubert's great song cycles, set to poetry by Wilhelm Müller. *The Well-Tempered Clavier* is a set of solo keyboard music composed by Johann Sebastian Bach.

15 Under National Socialism, being asocial (*asozial*) – a term that covered not only refusing to work (being work shy) but also non-conformist behaviour in general – had also been criminalized.

16 In East Germany, such state-owned firms were officially known as the "People's Own Enterprises" (*volkseigene Betriebe*, or VEBs).

16 That is, East Berlin and the rural region surrounding it (Brandenburg).

16 Kuczynski is making a pun here on the GDR anthem, "Auferstanden aus Ruinen" (Risen from Ruins), whose first line runs: "Auferstanden aus Ruinen, *und der Zukunft zugewandt*, laßt uns Dir zum Guten dienen, Deutschland, einig Vaterland" (Risen from ruins *and facing the future*, let us serve you for the good, Germany, united fatherland).

17 Friedrich Hölderlin (1770–1843), Friedrich Schiller (1759–1805), Heinrich von Kleist (1777–1811), Georg Büchner (1813–1837), and Joseph von Eichendorff (1788–1857) were all major German writers, known especially for their poetry and plays.

18 A meat-based roulade consists of a slice of meat rolled around a filling (of cheese, vegetables, other meats like bacon, etc.) that is then covered with wine or stock and cooked. After cooking, the roulade is sliced and served. It is, in short, a savory version of the popular jelly roll.

18 Jagdwurst and Thüringer are popular types of German sausages.

20 In many parts of the world, May First is celebrated as the international day of labour.

21 Made in East Germany for some thirty years, the Trabant was the most common automobile on East Germany's roads and streets.

23 In East Germany, the practice of building using prefabricated slabs was called *Plattenbau*.

23 Bertolt Brecht was a leading twentieth-century German dramatist and socialist intellectual, famous for such works as *The Threepenny Opera*, *Mother Courage*, and *The Caucasian Chalk Circle*. During the years of Nazi rule he lived in exile first in Scandinavia and then the United States, but he returned to Germany in 1948, taking up residence in East Berlin.

27 Interhotel was the name of an East German hotel chain founded in the 1960s, which tended to cater to guests from non-communist countries.

27 Kuczynski employs the phrase "coloured light" here to avoid the more common "red light," which in East Germany referred not only to drugs and prostitution (e.g., a "red light" district) but also to "socialist illumination" or propaganda.

29 In Germany, homosexual relations between men were first declared criminal in 1871 under Paragraph 175 of the Penal Code. During the Nazi era, the law was broadened and penalties for breaking it made much more severe. These Nazi additions were repealed by the East German government in 1950, but homosexual relations between men remained a crime there until 1968.

30 That is, in the rural area surrounding Berlin. Brandenburg State (Mark Brandenburg) was the name given to the lands of the former Prussian province of Brandenburg, excluding those situated east of the Oder-Neisse line (which were ceded to Poland in 1946). This territorial unit, however, disappeared in 1952 when the East German government decided to reorganize the country's five states into a group of fourteen administrative districts (*Bezirke*).

31 In communist states, the word "nomenklatura" referred to a list of qualified individuals, drawn up by Communist Party leaders, who could be appointed to vacant senior positions in the Party, state, and other important organizations. It thus refers to the state and Party bureaucracies.

32 Wandlitz was a village lying about thirty kilometres northeast of Berlin. In 1958, GDR authorities constructed a secured residential community for East Germany's political and military elite just outside the village. Until reunification, this *Waldsiedlung* (or "forest settlement") was strictly off-limits to all ordinary citizens.

34 "Es brennt, Brüder, es brennt" or "S'Brent" (It Burns) is the most famous song of the important Yiddish musician and songwriter Mordechai

Gebirtig (1877–1942). It was written in 1938 to commemorate the 1936 pogrom in the Polish village of Przytyk, and was often sung in the Jewish ghettos of Nazi-occupied Europe. "Sag nie" was composed in 1943 by Hirsh Glick in the Vilna Ghetto. During the war, it served as the anthem for several Jewish partisan brigades; thereafter, it became one of the chief anthems of Holocaust survivors. Aaron Zeitlin (words) and Sholom Secunda (music) wrote "Dana Dana" (in English Donna Donna) for New York's Yiddish theatre in 1940–1.

35 The *keffieyeh* is a traditional Arab head covering made from a square of cotton cloth. Associated with Palestinian culture, it became a powerful symbol of Palestinian identity and solidarity after PLO leader Yasser Arafat started wearing one in the 1960s.

35 Here Kuczynski refers to the phrase "real existierender Sozialismus" (real existing socialism), which from the late 1960s on was frequently used by Party figures to describe the existence of a real, functioning socialist society in the present.

36 "The construction of socialism" (*Aufbau des Sozialismus*) was a phrase and political program closely associated with the regime of Walter Ulbricht, who led the DDR from 1950 until 1971. The program was officially announced in 1952 at the Second Party Congress of the SED.

36 The "International" is one of the most famous anthems of the socialist and (later) communist movements.

36 Nikolai Ostrokovsky (1904–1936) was a Soviet socialist realist writer. Although it was the only novel he completed, *How the Steel Was Tempered* earned him considerable renown, and this passage, in particular, was regularly memorized by communist faithful around the world.

38 This sentence appears in a section devoted to the concept of alienation in the seventh (of seven) notebooks that comprise Marx's *Grundrisse*.

40 There were two kinds of personal cars made in East Germany, the Wartburg and the Trabant (or Trabi). The Wartburg was the larger and more comfortable of the two.

40 Knorr and Maggi were popular brands for food products produced in West Germany; these products were not readily available in East Germany.

42 This was the slogan that the Czechoslovakian communist leader, Alexander Dubček, used in 1968 to characterize the political reform program that became known as the Prague Spring. This experiment in political liberalization under communist rule was brutally ended on

21 August 1968 when the Soviet Union and members of the Warsaw Pact invaded Czechoslovakia.

42 "Automatic firing devices" or *Selbstschussanlage* was the official name given in East Germany to the antipersonnel installations (SM-70s) deployed along the border separating East from West Germany, starting in 1970. Although it was discussed at one time, these devices were never deployed on the Berlin Wall.

47 In Hegelian terminology, *Seinslogik.*

49 "Developed socialism" or *entwickelter Sozialismus* was a concept that emerged in the 1960s and then became part of official SED ideology in 1971. It posited that socialism was a specific stage of historical development in the transition to full communism.

52 This quotation is actually drawn from two different texts. The first part comes from a middle section of "Systemfragment von 1800" (Fragment of a System), and the second comes at the end of "Religion, eine Religion stiften," from G.W.F. Hegel, *Werke in zwanzig Bänden*, vol. 1 *Frühschriften* (Frankfurt am Main: Suhrkamp Verlag, 1971), respectively 419–27 and 239–41, here 422 and 241.

55 Gottfried Wilhelm von Leibniz (1646–1716), a noted philosopher and mathematician (he published his discovery of differential calculus some nine years before Isaac Newton), is regarded as one of Germany's greatest minds. The brothers Humboldt, Alexander (1769–1859) and Wilhelm (1767–1835), were major intellectual and academic figures in the early part of the nineteenth century. Alexander made his fame as a scientific traveller, mineralogist, and botanist (spending some five years in South America), while Wilhelm was prominent as a statesman during the German reform era and as the founder of the University of Berlin.

57 A favourite German card game, normally played among three people.

57 The phrase "pure reason" refers to the title of Immanuel Kant's noted work, *Critique of Pure Reason.*

57 Along with the Staatsoper (Unter den Linden), the Komische Oper was one of two opera companies in East Berlin. The specialty of the Komische Oper, as its name suggests, was comic opera and operetta; all productions there are performed in German.

58 Here Kuczynski is paraphrasing a passage that occurs in the opening section of Marx's *German Ideology* (1845). The complete line reads: "… in communist society, where nobody has one exclusive sphere of activity but each can become accomplished in any branch he wishes, society regulates

the general production and thus makes it possible for me to do one thing today and another tomorrow, to hunt in the morning, fish in the afternoon, rear cattle in the evening, criticize after dinner, just as I have a mind, without ever becoming hunter, fisherman, herdsman or critic" (part I.A. section 4).

64 The painter Max Liebermann (1847–1935) was a founder of the fin-de-siècle avant-garde Berlin "Sezession" movement and became a leading exponent of Impressionism in Germany.

64 Anne-Robert-Jacques Turgot (1727–1781) was a noted French public figure and economist. A man of the French Enlightenment and contributor to the *Encyclopédie,* he promoted a number of economic reforms as Louis XV's comptroller-general of finances from 1774 to 1776.

64 Supported by the Soviet leader, Leonid Brezhnev, Erich Honecker engineered a bloodless coup in 1971 to replace Walter Ulbricht as First Secretary of the SED, making him the *de facto* head of East Germany.

64 Käthe Kollwitz (1867–1945) was a German painter, printmaker, and sculptor. Much of her most famous work focuses on the human condition, especially the plight of those suffering from poverty, war, and hunger.

66 Born in Budapest and educated in Vienna, Arthur Koestler (1905–1983) achieved fame as journalist and, later, as a novelist. He joined the Communist Party in the early 1930s and in 1936 went to Spain to cover the Civil War. His experiences there, however, caused him to renounce Soviet-style communism. From the late 1930s on, much of his literary output, including *Darkness at Noon,* sought to expose communism's lies and shortcomings, including its history of political show trials and purges.

67 The "socialist human community" (*sozialistische Menschengemeinschaft*) was an social ideal put forth by Ulbricht in the 1960s, according to which people were to live together in harmony, free from exploitation and, consequently, social conflict.

73 The original German reads: "Nachts weint der Clown, erblindet fast vom Rampenlicht / findet er im Tageslicht / gangbare Wege nicht, / allein auf Nebelgleisen / versucht er durch die Stadt zu schleichen / doch Spiegelketten überall / …"

76 A long-time activist in Chile's Socialist Party, Salvador Allende became the country's democratically elected president in 1970. Opposition to his policies, both from far-right groups in Chile and from the United States government, led to a constitutional crisis, and, on 11 September 1973, General Augusto Pinochet led a successful coup against the Allende regime. Allende himself died in the conflict, and many of his supporters fled into exile.

77 In the original, Kuczynski mistakenly spells the hotel name "Johanneshof."

78 The word "Politbürokratie" (translated here as "Politbureaucracy") reflects East Germans' dry wit. Created by combining "Politburo" with "bureaucracy," the word implies that the organization that should be promoting world revolution (the Politburo) behaves more as part of the established order (the bureaucracy).

78 This is a reference to the so-called "Song of the Party," composed in 1949 by the Bohemian communist Louis Fürnberg, whose refrain began with the words "The Party, the Party is always right" (Die Partei, die Partei, die hat immer recht).

80 Starting in 1964, the East German government agreed to let political prisoners and other East Germans (frequently people cut off from their families) emigrate in exchange for payment (ransom) by the West German government. Altogether some 250,000 individuals left East Germany through this process, officially called "Freikauf" (the buying of freedom), but denounced by some in the West as a form of human trafficking. The politics and controversies surrounding this practice are well explored in an article by Maximilian Horster, "The Trade in Political Prisoners between the Two German States, 1962–1989," *Journal of Contemporary History* 39 (2004): 403–24.

82 The Palace of the Republic (Palast der Republik) was the building on the Unter den Linden where the East German Parliament met and other cultural activities were held. Built on the site of the former city palace of the Prussian royal family (the Hohenzollern) between 1973 and 1976, the building was torn down between 2006 and 2008.

82 Kurt Hager (1912–1998) was a key figure in the East German Communist Party throughout the postwar era. In 1949 he was tapped to lead the SED's Propaganda Department, and in 1955 became a secretary in the SED Central Committee, where he was responsible for science, popular education, and cultural affairs. He joined the East German Politburo in 1963, where, until the collapse of the regime in 1989, he functioned as East Germany's chief ideologist.

83 In 1956, the West German government voted to ban the Communist Party of Germany (KPD). In 1968, a group of West German communists founded the German Communist Party (DKP) as the KPD's successor.

89 Günter Mittag (1926–1994) was a leading figure in the formation of East German economic policy, becoming in 1976 secretary for the economy within the SED Central Committee.

91 Having fled the Nazis in 1936, Stephan Hermlin (1915–1997) returned to Germany in 1945, moving to East Berlin two years later. There the

talented journalist and writer established himself as one of East Germany's foremost literary figures, counting among his friends both Walter Ulbricht and Erich Honecker.

92 Germans typically use the term "die Wende" (transition, turn) to refer to the collapse of the East German communist regime.

93 The book fair at Frankfurt am Main, held each year in October, is the world's largest trade show devoted to books and book publishing.

96 Pablo Neruda (1904–1973) was one of Chile's most famous poets and received the Nobel Prize for literature in 1971. Active in Communist Party politics for much of his life, Neruda died of heart failure in Santiago just days after Salvador Allende's socialist government was overthrown in the coup led by Augusto Pinochet.

98 Along with Diego Rivera, David Alfaro Siqueiros (1896–1974) and José Clemente Orózco (1883–1949) were the founders of the modern school of Mexican mural painting, noted above all for its bold compositions and use of colours as well as the monumental scale of its creations.

98 Violeta Parra (1917–1967) was a Chilean composer, folk singer, and social activist, best known as a co-founder of the *Nueva Canción* (new song) movement that helped revolutionize Chilean popular music in the late 1960s and early 1970s. Victor Lidio Jara (1932–1973) was a Chilean theatre director, singer-songwriter, political activist, and member of the Communist Party, as well an influential figure in the *Nueva Canción* movement. Soon after the overthrow of Allende's government on 11 September 1973, Jara was arrested, tortured, and ultimately shot dead. Formed in 1967, Inti-Illimani is a Chilean folk music ensemble who became an especially well known exponent of the *Nueva Canción* movement. On tour in Europe when the anti-Allende coup occurred, the group continued to perform in exile and worked on behalf of Chilean democracy, returning to Chile only in September 1988.

100 This was the Stasi's formal term for its informants.

101 The general secretary of the SED was the *de facto* head of the East German state.

102 Milovan Djilas (1911–1995) was a Yugoslav politican, theorist, and author, active both in the Yugoslavian partisan movement during the Second World War and in the postwar government. A proponent of "democratic socialism," in the years after 1949 he promoted a more free-thinking position that put him afoul of the Yugoslav Communist Party. In 1954, he was expelled from the Party for publishing

the essays (in the Party's newspaper) about the emergence of a new ruling "class" under communism, which were later republished in the West as *The New Class*. Jailed repeatedly between 1955 and 1966, Djilas continued his dissident activities until the collapse of Yugoslav communist rule in the 1980s.

102 Two small towns southeast of Berlin.

103 Wladimir Wladimirowitsch Majakowski (1893–1930) was a Georgian/ Russian poet, a major figure in the Russian branch of the Futurist art movement, and after 1917 a leading literary figure *cum* political agitator in the Soviet Union. In 1950, the East Berlin government decided to name an ellipse-shaped street in the Pankow district after him, namely Majakowskiring, which lay in the centre of the protected neighbourhood established for the GDR's VIPs.

104 KaDeWe is short for "Kaufhaus des Westens," literally the "department store of the West." Founded in 1905 and located in what became West Berlin, after 1945 it became one of the largest shopping centres in Western Europe and an icon of West German (i.e., capitalist) material prosperity.

104 Maximilien Robespierre was a leading figure in the radical phase of the French Revolution. The Convention was the name given to the French National Assembly elected in the late summer of 1792, which in September 1793 authorized "terror" becoming the order of the day.

107 Kuczynski actually writes "the checkpoint for entering and leaving the GDR." While this is accurate (East Berlin was after all the capital of East Germany), it seemed clearer in this context to substitute East Berlin for the GDR.

107 Between 1962 and 1989, the Friedrichsstrasse station was the primary border crossing point for Germans travelling between East and West Germany. The expression "Palace of Tears" (*Tränenpalast*) refers to the tears frequently shed as East Germans said their goodbyes in front of the station building to their friends and family returning back to West Berlin.

108 The district of Steglitz lies in south-central West Berlin.

109 Here Kuczynski refers to a notion, the society of niches or *Nischengesellschaft*, that the former West German emissary to the GDR, Guenter Gaus, had proposed in 1983 as a way to understand aspects of East German social life. Once prominent in analyses of East German society, the term has now been largely abandoned by scholars.

110 Meant here is the "New" Synagogue on the Oranienburger Strasse. Built between 1859 and 1866 as the main synagogue for Berlin's Jewish community, the structure was ransacked and set on fire on the Night of Broken Glass (or *Kristallnacht*, 9–10 November 1938); saved from total destruction in 1938, it was devastated by the Allied bombing raids on Berlin in 1943 and 1944.

118 Rudolf Bahro (1935–1997) was a German journalist, Communist Party functionary, and one-time East German bureaucrat. His provocative book, *The Alternative in Eastern Europe: An Analysis of Actually-Existing Socialism* (1977), so incensed GDR authorities that he was arrested in 1977 and sentenced to eight years in prison. After an international outcry he was released and exiled to West Germany in October 1979, where he became a leader in the nascent Green Party.

121 Intershop was a chain of state-owned retail stores in East Germany, where high-quality Western goods, normally unavailable elsewhere in the country, could be purchased with hard currency.

124 Kuczynski gives the date as 1974, but the Accords were indeed signed in 1975.

125 This anniversary celebration was, in fact, a major political event, arguably the most important state commemoration in the GDR's entire history.

125 On 2 May 1989, the Hungarian government boldly decided to begin dismantling its 240-kilometre-long border fence with Austria, which allowed East Germans on vacation there to escape relatively easily to the West.

125 The Märkische Schweiz is a hilly area in Brandenburg some thirty kilometres east of Berlin.

126 That is, when Honecker visited Bonn in 1987.

127 ARD and ZDF were the two state-owned West German television channels.

130 Held on 18 March 1990.

130 Alexander Schalck-Golodkowski was a key figure in the GDR's foreign trade activities for most of his career. Already in 1956, he was named a department director in the Ministry for Foreign Trade. In 1966, he became the head of the important "Commercial Coordination" department in the same ministry, serving there for twenty years until joining the SED's Central Committee in 1986.

130 Elected to the Volkskammer as a CDU deputy in March 1990, Lothar de Maizière was named to head the East German government as premier in April, making him the last person to hold the position.

130 In West Germany, the Post Office (Bundespost) held a complete monopoly over both telephone and postal services until 1996.

133 As a result of their exposure to Stalinism, Leonhard, Koestler, and Sperber all become disillusioned with communism and wrote publicly about their change of heart.

133 Namely, the essay Koestler contributed (in English) to Richard H.S. Crossman's *The God That Failed* (1949).

134 In referring to the two parts of the Federal Republic post-unification, it is customary to use "east" and "west" rather than "East" and "West" (and their respective variants). Hence the switch here to the lowercase "w."

136 The Delikat (launched in 1966) and Exquisit (1962) stores were chains that sought to provide higher-quality goods to East Germans, albeit at inflated prices. Delikat was a sort of upscale grocery, while Exquisit sold clothing and cosmetics.

136 Forum cheques were a type of foreign exchange voucher, valued at the rate of 1 "Forum mark" to the DM, with which East Germans could purchase goods in the Intershops.

138 That is, those of Kuczynski's friends who had been active in the West German protest movements of 1968.

138 A member of the Moscow-based group led by Walter Ulbricht charged with organizing the administration of Soviet-occupied Germany (the future German Democratic Republic), Wolfgang Leonhard fled to Yugoslavia in 1949 when it became clear that East Germany, under Ulbricht, was to become a Stalinist satellite state. Soon after its release in 1955, *Child of the Revolution* (in German, *Die Revolution entlässt ihre Kinder*) was recognized as a brilliant account of the dark side of Stalinist rule in Eastern Europe.

138 The term "Frankfurt School" refers to school of interdisciplinary social thought and analysis associated with the Institute for Social Research, founded in the Weimar Republic at the University of Frankfurt am Main. Established as a centre for research in philosophy and the social sciences from a Marxist (although non-communist) perspective, under the leadership of Max Horkheimer, the Institute developed influential theories of aesthetics (Theodor Adorno and Walter Benjamin) as well as critiques of capitalist culture. Although the National Socialists shut down the Institute in 1933, many members continued their work in exile in the United States. In 1949, the Institute was reestablished in Frankfurt, where Jürgen Habermas became one of its most noted figures.

144 Until 1977, Marzahn was a largely rural area within the boundaries of East Berlin. In that year, East German authorities began constructing massive housing projects there to overcome overcrowding elsewhere in the city. Altogether the Marzahn development comprised some one hundred thousand apartments in the houses made of prefabricated concrete slabs (*Plattenbau*).

147 The Berliner Ensemble was a prominent East German theatre company founded by the playwright Bertolt Brecht (see note to p. 23, above), which has its home at the Theater "Am Schiffbauerdamm" in Berlin-Mitte.

153 The "solidarity contribution" or Solidaritätszuschlag (Kuczynski, however, uses the term "Solidarbeitrag") was introduced in 1991 as a supplemental tax on (initially, "west") German incomes in order to pay the economic and social costs of German unification. In particular, the tax financed the creation of a special "solidarity pact," through which billions of German marks (after 2001, euros) have funnelled into the "new" Federal states (aka old East Germany) from what had been West Germany.

153 That is, the American, British, and French occupation zones of Germany.

155 Ingeborg Bachmann (1926–1973) was a distinguished Austrian poet and author, whose work focused on such themes as personal boundaries, the establishment of truth, and the philosophy of language. This quote comes from the address Bachmann gave in accepting the 1971 Anton Wildgans prize (a literary award given to a young or mid-career Austrian writer).

www.ingramcontent.com/pod-product-compliance
Ingram Content Group UK Ltd.
Pitfield, Milton Keynes, MK11 3LW, UK
UKHW032122310125
454513UK00004B/159

9 781442 616226